Developing Reading Comprehension Skills Years 3–4

Classic Poetry

Brilliant
PUBLICATIONS

Kate Heap

Publisher's information

We hope you and your pupils enjoy using the ideas in this book. Brilliant Publications publishes many other books to help primary school teachers. To find out more details on all of our titles, including those listed below, please go to our website: www.brilliantpublications.co.uk.

Books in the Developing Reading Comprehension Skills series:
Classic Poetry Years 3–4
Classic Poetry Years 5–6
Classic Children's Literature Years 3–4
Classic Children's Literature Years 5–6
Contemporary Children's Literature Years 3–4
Contemporary Children's Literature Years 5–6
Non-fiction Years 3–4
Non-fiction Years 5–6
Brilliant Activities for Reading Comprehension series
Getting to Grips with English Grammar series
Brilliant Activities for Creative Writing series
Brilliant Activities for Grammar and Punctuation series
Boost Creative Writing series

Published by Brilliant Publications Limited
Unit 10
Sparrow Hall Farm
Edlesborough
Dunstable
Bedfordshire
LU6 2ES, UK

www.brilliantpublications.co.uk

The name Brilliant Publications and the logo are registered trademarks.

Written by Kate Heap

© Brilliant Publications Limited 2021

Printed ISBN: 978-0-85747-853-5
ePDF ISBN: 978-0-85747-859-7
First printed in 2021

See pages 151–154 for Photograph credits and Acknowledgements.

Dedication

To the staff and students of Drighlington Junior School (2002 – 2004)
Creativity & Community

About the Author

Kate Heap

Kate has always loved books, her childhood overflowing with the adventures found within their pages. Now, as both a teacher and a parent, one of her greatest joys and privileges is sharing her love of literature with children.

Born and raised in Canada, Kate began her teaching career with Regina Public Schools. Ready for new adventures, she moved to the UK in 2001. Kate has spent many rewarding years in Leeds schools guiding children through the world of learning. She has supported primary school teachers through her roles of Literacy Leader, Leading Literacy Teacher for Leeds, Advanced Skills Teacher and Senior Leadership with responsibility for Assessment.

As a Primary English Consultant, Kate is now able to share her knowledge and enthusiasm even further. She enjoys reviewing children's literature for her blog, Scope for Imagination, working with authors and publishers to spread the word about their incredible books, and is passionate about helping teachers, parents and children find just the right ones for them. In her series, *Developing Reading Comprehension Skills*, Kate has created classroom resources that support both children and teachers in their quest to achieve key objectives and prepare for assessment while fostering a love of literature.

Kate is adventuring through life with her ever supportive husband, three wonderful children and two very special cats.

Contents

Introduction

Classic: Judged over a period of time to be of the highest quality and outstanding of its kind; a work of art of recognised and established value. (Oxford English Dictionary)

Why Classic Poems?

Classic poems are those which have stood the test of time. Their meaning is universal and timeless: as true now as it was when it was first written. Their language causes the reader to think and to feel. These poems take readers beyond their own circumstances and change how they see the world. Classic poems give the reader a window into the past, to another time or another place, while building empathy and understanding. These poems become a part of our shared language and tradition. When children learn these poems, they gain access to a common cultural language and an understanding of so many literary references.

The world of classic poetry is a place to escape. With the power to transform and change the way readers see the world, poetry can provide peace, inspiration, hope and focus. It opens up a world where playing with language is the norm and there is no one right answer. Children enjoy poetry for so many different reasons. They are able to explore language while gaining an awareness of words and their meaning. The musicality of poetry builds a sense of rhythm while developing emotional intelligence. Poems may be silly, funny or scary. They might address death, loss, remembrance, hope, love or joy. So much is expressed in so few words making them much more accessible than full novels. When reading a poem, children bring their own thoughts, experiences and emotions to the meaning making them intensely personal. Giving children the opportunity to learn these poems gives them the opportunity to find out more about themselves and the world around them.

In recent years, we have seen a number of changes to the Key Stage 2 English Curriculum, the Key Stage 2 Reading Test Framework and in the overall expectations for pupils. A focus on higher level vocabulary and increased use of more classic style texts and language has presented new challenges for both teachers and children. There is an expectation that children will have a strong understanding of a wide range of language devices. Poetry is the perfect avenue for exploring them.

In the Year 3 and 4 programme of study for reading comprehension in the National Curriculum, children are expected to develop many skills linked to poetry. These objectives from the National Curriculum outline just some of the links to poetry:

Pupils should be taught to maintain positive attitudes to reading and understanding of what they read by:

- listening to and discussing a wide range of fiction, poetry, plays, non-fiction and reference books or textbooks

- preparing poems and play scripts to read aloud and to perform, showing understanding through intonation, tone, volume and action

- recognising some different forms of poetry (for example, free verse, narrative poetry)

In addition, as children progress, they should meet texts of increasing complexity and challenge. Familiarity with a wide range of poems will help to develop many skills:

- identifying themes and conventions
- discussing words and phrases that capture the reader's interest and imagination
- checking the text makes sense to them, discussing their understanding and explaining the meaning of words in context
- drawing inferences and justifying inferences with evidence
- predicting what might happen
- summarising main ideas
- identifying structure.

It is essential that children become familiar with the wealth of classic poetry from both Great Britain and other countries. The richness of language and universality of themes provided by these types of texts allow children to expand their understanding of the world. They are then better able to make links between literature, history, geography, science and other areas.

In this book, children in Lower Key Stage 2 (Years 3 and 4) are exposed to a range of these rich poems. It is just a small sample of the thousands of wonderful poems that teachers and children may wish to read and study. Through these poems, children are given opportunities to tackle more complex vocabulary and widen their knowledge of synonyms, develop understanding of challenging language devices and practise each of the eight Reading Content Domain question types. It is also my hope that children will want to read more poetry and have the opportunity to discover some of the greatest poems ever written.

As a part of the *Developing Reading Comprehension Skills* series, this book would also be appropriate for children in Upper Key Stage 2 (Years 5 and 6) who would benefit from less complex texts, lower level vocabulary or more support in developing answers.

The poems selected for this book have been intentionally chosen to provide teachers with a variety of poets, topics and themes. This broadens the range of children's reading and ensures there will be something of interest for every reader.

Female Poets: UK
Christina Rossetti: Boats Sail on the Rivers, England, 1872
Female Poets: International
Emily Dickinson: A Bird, Came Down the Walk, USA, 1891
Lucy Maud Montgomery: Night, Canada, 1935
Rachel Field: Something Told the Wild Geese, USA, 1934
May Swenson: The Cloud-Mobile, USA, 1958
Effie Lee Newsome: The Bronze Legacy, USA, 1922

Male Poets: UK
Robert Louis Stevenson: My Shadow, Scotland, 1885
A.A. Milne: Buckingham Palace, England, 1924
Edward Lear: The Owl and the Pussy-Cat, England, 1871
Alfred, Lord Tennyson: The Eagle, England, 1851
Male Poets: International
Clement Clarke Moore: A Visit from St. Nicholas, USA, 1823
Vachel Lindsay: The Flower-Fed Buffaloes, USA, 1926

Publication Date	Poem Title & Author	Theme
1823	A Visit from St. Nicholas by *Clement Clarke Moore*	Christmas, Wonder, Magic
1851	The Eagle by *Alfred, Lord Tennyson*	Nature, Beauty, Power, Strength
1871	The Owl and the Pussy-Cat by *Edward Lear*	Nonsense, Joy, Love and Marriage
1872	Boats Sail on the Rivers by *Christina Rossetti*	Nature, Human Impact, Beauty
1885	My Shadow by *Robert Louis Stevenson*	Childhood, Science, Experimenting, Curiosity
1891	A Bird, Came Down the Walk by *Emily Dickinson*	Beauty of Nature, Wonder at Nature, Respect
1922	The Bronze Legacy by *Effie Lee Newsome*	Celebrating Self, Acceptance, Beauty, Strength, Respect
1924	Buckingham Palace by *A.A. Milne*	Empathy, Royal Duties
1926	The Flower-Fed Buffaloes by *Vachel Lindsay*	Nature, Colonisation, Conservation, Progress
1934	Something Told the Wild Geese by *Rachel Field*	Autumn, Nature, Migration, Changes, Seasons
1935	Night by *Lucy Maud Montgomery*	Nature, Night, Dealing with Troubles, Solitude, Comfort
1958	The Cloud-Mobile by *May Swenson*	Nature, Earth is Always Changing, Cycles

How to use this book

Reading, understanding, writing and performing poetry should be a key part of any school's English curriculum. Exposure to this wonderful style of writing is so important and must not be just an add-on. Key poems must be carefully selected and built into a broad plan for English so children do not miss out on these important experiences. The poems and questions in this book can be easily used as the skeleton for some of these poetry units and then be built up with further activities in the classroom.

The poems in this book are ordered from easier to more difficult. Teachers may wish to use them in this order, select poems linked to class topics/themes or choose those they think will most interest the class.

The content domain question types are organised in the order in which they appear in the National Curriculum but it is important that teachers think about the needs of their class and choose content domains accordingly. Teachers may wish to begin with more basic retrieval before moving on to more difficult content domains such as vocabulary or author's use of language. You will notice there are more vocabulary, retrieval, inference and author's use of language questions than the other content domains. This reflects the weighting of the question types in the KS2 Reading SATs papers, the nature of the poems and gives children more opportunities to practise these skills.

The poems and questions have been designed to work well within a variety of teaching styles: whole class sessions, smaller teacher-led sessions or child-led groups. They may be used as a supported or independent task. The flexibility of this resource means it can be used in many different ways. Children in Year 3 or with less developed skills may benefit from reading and discussing the texts together with an adult before moving on to the questions.

Each unit, consisting of a poem and eight question types, should be taught over a number of sessions, allowing the teacher time to really focus on the strategies needed to answer each question type. These units should be used as taught lessons rather than as assessment tools as there is so much scope for discussion to deepen children's understanding of the language and themes. No matter how the units are used, children should always finish with reading through the poem again so they can apply everything they have learned and gain a deeper understanding of the meaning as a whole.

Some of the poems are more difficult in language, length or content. However, the accompanying questions have been designed to guide children through the texts and help them to develop their comprehension and reading skills. All of the poems have been trialled by Key Stage 2 children. They found that, at first, the poems seemed quite difficult but once they worked through the questions, they understood what the poems were about, had learned a lot of new vocabulary and gained insights into the meaning. This level of challenge is helpful for children and gives them opportunity to experience how language has changed over time.

Poetry Toolkit

Before children begin to read these poems, it is important that they have an understanding of their "Poetry Toolkit". This is the collection of poetic (language) devices used in poems to create images and meaning. I like to encourage children to keep these "tools" with them whenever they read poetry so they are ready to make connections and build their understanding. You may wish to display these tools in the classroom or even create a toolbox with real or play tools labelled with each poetic device.

Tool	Meaning
Imagery	The creation of mental images through description
Simile	Comparing one thing to another by saying it is "like" or "as" that other thing
Metaphor	Something that represents or is a symbol of something else. The characteristics of one thing are similar to the characteristics of another
Personification	Giving a human characteristic to an inanimate object, animal or abstract concept
Alliteration	Repetition of the same initial sound in closely located words
Assonance	Repetition of the same vowel sound in the middle of closely located words
Consonance	Repetition of the same consonant sound in the middle of closely located words
Repetition	Repeating the same word or phrase for effect
Onomatopoeia	A word that imitates the sound it is describing (eg, pop)
Rhythm	The flow of a poem including the pattern or beat created by the syllables and stressed sounds in a line of poetry
Rhyme	Repetition of the ending sounds of words (often at the end of lines of poetry)

Using Poems in the Classroom

The richness of these poems provides endless classroom opportunities. Rather than just reading and analysing the stand-alone poems, teachers and their students may wish to bring them to life through further exploration together. Take advantage of the seasons and special days to read appropriate poems: autumn, spring, Christmas… there are so many links to be made with poetry. Poems learned around days that are special to children are likely to be remembered and recalled when these special occasions come around again in the future.

Children may be inspired to write in a similar style or use the content of the poem to inspire their own compositions across a range of genres and purposes. The best writing often comes from meaningful classroom activities based on high-quality texts.

The classic poems in this book lend themselves to a whole host of teaching activities. I would encourage teachers to use these texts as a springboard to jump off into further learning.

- Speaking and listening activities such as expressing opinions, questioning, description, persuasion and debate
- Learn poems by heart and for performance
- Drama activities such as role play, hot seating, freeze-frame and characterisation
- Explore different styles of poetry. Which do the children prefer: narrative, sonnet, haiku, rhyme or no rhyme?
- Examine how poetry "breaks the rules" of punctuation and grammar
- Compare perspectives on the same topic. Look at contrasting poems by the same or different authors. Does everyone see things the same way? This could be a simple comparison of descriptions of nature or a more complex analysis of opinions about exploration and settlement
- Historical research into the author, time period, technology, links to historical events, comparisons between time periods or a related educational visit
- Biographies of authors or historical characters
- Geographical research into the setting location, study of geographical features (eg, islands, mountains, seas) and map drawing
- ICT links such as computer animation, short films, reviews, advertisements and recording their own poems complete with sound effects
- Explore how painting, drawing or sculpture might represent the poem
- Use physical movement (dance or gymnastics) to interpret the meaning
- Poem to video comparisons (There are many animated versions of classic poems)
- Read a "Poem a Day" to expose children to a wide range of poems – both classic and more contemporary
- Watch poetry videos: Michael Rosen, Shel Silverstein and The Poetry Foundation website are just a few examples of fantastic videos available

Follow the children's lead. With some poems, they will be happy to read, practise the question types and move on while other poems will capture their imaginations and natural curiosity. Grab this and run with it! They may be whisked away into the nonsense of *The Owl and the Pussy-Cat* or enchanted by the setting of *Night*. They might be intrigued by *The Cloud-Mobile* or struck by the meaning of *The Bronze Legacy*. Take time to explore and develop their curiosity. It will inspire a life-long love of poetry.

Reading Content Domain

Vocabulary

Give or explain the meaning of words in context.

The **Vocabulary** content domain is not only about the words children know but also the strategies they possess for working out the meaning of words they don't know. Children must use the context of the surrounding line, stanza or entire poem to work out the meaning of the words. By thinking about what has been happening in the poem so far and searching for clues, children are able to learn new words and expand their vocabulary. This content domain draws heavily on children's understanding of synonyms and their ability to use the "replacement method" in which they remove the word in question and replace it with each option in turn to find the best fit.

Example: **The Owl and the Pussy-Cat**

In the question below, replace "tarried" with each option to find the best fit answer.

"O let us be married! too long we have tarried:"

Which word is closest in meaning to "tarried"?

	Tick **one**
rushed	
waited	
dated	
sung	

Retrieval

Retrieve and record information / identify key details from fiction and non-fiction.

The **Retrieval** content domain is about children being able to find key pieces of information in the poem. Using keywords and a highlighting strategy will help children to make links between the key words in the question and similar wording in the poem. By scanning the poem, they can spot the keywords, highlight them and find their answer. It is important to note that it may not be the exact wording from the question in the poem. Synonyms may be used.

Example: **A Visit from St. Nicholas**
In the question below, the keywords are up and chimney. Once children find these words (or synonyms for them) in the poem, they will be able to find the answer.

How did St. Nicholas get back up the chimney?

Summary

Summarise main ideas from more than one paragraph.

The *Summary* content domain is about children being able to sum up or condense what they have read. This may involve identifying the key points of the poem or coming up with an appropriate heading for a stanza. In these questions, more than one answer may be correct, but children must choose what they believe to be the best or most appropriate answer and then justify their choice. Discussion about the different options is key to help children understand that many poems have more than one theme.

Example: **The Flower-Fed Buffaloes**

In the question below, children are asked to identify the main idea/lesson of the entire poem. They need to choose the answer that provides the best overall meaning.

What is the main message of the poem?

	Tick **one**
There have been positive changes on the prairie.	
Progress has caused beautiful things of the past to vanish.	
Change is a bad thing.	
Progress and development is good.	

Inference

Make inferences from the text / explain and justify inferences with evidence from the text.

The *Inference* content domain is about children being detectives and looking for clues in the poem to support their answers. It is important for them to remember that whenever they make a point (or give an answer), they also need to provide a quote from or reference to the poem that proves what they are saying.

Example: **Something Told the Wild Geese**

In the question below, children need to decide whether their answer is yes or no then find a quote in the text that proves their answer. In this case, they are looking for the fact that the ice was "remembered". The space for the answer is structured for the children to encourage them to provide evidence.

Have the geese experienced ice before? How do you know?

_____ because _____

_____

Prediction

Predict what might happen from details stated and implied.

The **Prediction** content domain is about making logical or reasonable predictions about what might happen later in the poem. Children should be able to back up their ideas with evidence from the poem or knowledge about the time period that has led them to believe in their predictions.

> Example: **Buckingham Palace**
>
> In the question below, children need to develop an understanding of the time in which this poem is set. The fact that Alice is Christopher Robin's nanny and she is getting married means that she will no longer be able to care for him and take him on outings all the time.
>
> What will happen to Alice and Christopher Robin's outings to see the changing of the guard once she gets married? Why?

Text Meaning

Identify/explain how information/narrative content is related and contributes to meaning as a whole.

The **Text Meaning** content domain is about identifying the structural and language features of the poem and understanding the role of each part of the poem. This includes explaining how certain parts of a poem help to create or change the overall meaning.

> Example: **The Eagle**
> In the question below, children are required to match each feature of the poem with an example.
>
> Draw lines to match each poetic technique with the correct quotation from the text.
>
> | | |
> |---|---|
> | hyperbole | And like a thunderbolt he falls. |
> | alliteration | He clasps the crag with crooked hands; |
> | rhyme | The wrinkled sea beneath him crawls; He watches from his mountain walls, |
> | simile | Close to the sun |

In poetry, there will also be questions about the rhyme scheme and rhythm of the poem.

Children may be asked to identify the pattern of the rhyme. Each new sound at the end of a line is assigned a different letter. The rhyme scheme might be in couplets (AABB) or alternate rhyme (ABAB).

The rhythm of the poem is the beat or syllables in each line. Children will need to consider the number of syllables, line length and how these affect how the poem sounds.

Example: **Something Told the Wild Geese**

What is the rhyme scheme of this poem. **Tick one**.

ABBA		ABCD	
ABCB		ABAB	

The rhythm of this poem is very consistent. What is the pattern of <u>syllables</u> in each <u>stanza</u>? **Tick one**.

5-5-5-5		6-5-6-5	
5-6-7-8		7-8-7-8	

Think about what this poem is about. What does this consistent rhythm remind you of?

Author's Use of Language

Identify/explain how meaning is enhanced through choice of words and phrases.

The *Author's Use of Language* content domain is about children recognising figurative language and descriptive phrases that contribute to the overall meaning of the poem. Once children spot these features, they need to both understand what the features mean and identify the impact on the reader. There are various strategies children may use to answer these types of questions.

a) <u>Mind Map method</u> – Children identify the keyword in the question and place it at the centre of a mind map (spider diagram). They then write down everything they know about the word. Once they have thought through all of the possible meanings or associations of the word, they choose the most logical or best fit ideas to create their answer. If there is more than one word identified in the question, children should make sure they include an explanation or reference to each word in their answer.

Example: **Something Told the Wild Geese**

"Something told the wild geese"

What does the phrase <u>wild geese</u> tell the reader about these animals?

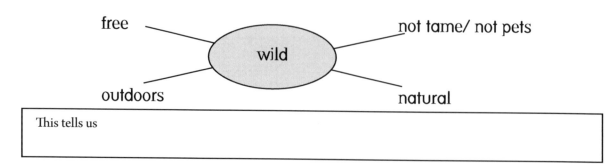

free — not tame/ not pets

wild

outdoors — natural

This tells us

b) <u>Replacement method</u> as described in the **Vocabulary** content domain.

c) <u>Identify figurative language techniques</u> (simile, metaphor, imagery, personification etc) and write about how the author is using that technique.

Example: **A Bird, Came Down the Walk**
In the question below, children use their knowledge about similes (comparison phrases beginning with "like" or "as") to spot the simile in the poem ("like frightened Beads"). They then must give an explanation of how the comparison helps the reader to picture the bird's eyes.

Find and **copy a simile** that describes the bird's eyes.

_____

What does this <u>simile</u> tell the reader about the bird's eyes?

_____

_____

Compare and Contrast

Make comparisons within the text.

The **Comparison** content domain is about children identifying how characters, settings, events or moods in a poem are similar to or different from each other. It also requires children to identify how a character changes over the course of a poem. When answering these questions, children must choose the most appropriate conjunction to link their ideas together as they build their answer.

To Show Similarity / Compare	To Show Difference / Contrast
similarly	but
also	however
in addition	on the other hand
in the same way	whereas
they are both…	while
likewise	yet
equally	unlike

Example: **The Bronze Legacy**

In the question below, children are asked to identify how the wren and eagle are different. The use of contrasting conjunctions makes the answer very clear.

The reader then needs to think about why the poet used these contrasting images to help communicate their message.

In the second stanza, the poet describes a wren and an eagle. How are they different?
A wren is a small, fragile bird but/however an eagle is very large and strong.

What does this difference tell the reader about being brown?
The poet is telling the reader that things which are brown come in all shapes and sizes but each one is important.

Boats Sail on the Rivers

by Christina Rossetti

Boats sail on the rivers,

And ships sail on the seas;

But clouds that sail across the sky

Are prettier far than these.

There are bridges on the rivers,

As pretty as you please;

But the bow that bridges heaven,

And overtops the trees,

And builds a road from earth to sky,

Is prettier far than these.

Vocabulary   Boats Sail on the Rivers

1. **Find** and **copy two words** that are bodies of water.

1. _____

2. _____

2. "*Are prettier far than these.*"
Circle the **best synonym** for <u>prettier</u>.

uglier	higher
fluffier	lovelier

3. Look at the entire poem. **Find** and **copy another word** for sky.

_____

4. Look at the entire poem. **Find** and **copy a word** that could be replaced with <u>above</u>.

_____

5. Look at the entire poem. **Find** and **copy a synonym** for <u>constructs</u>.

_____

Boats Sail on the Rivers

1. Where do boats and ships sail?

_____

2. Which image best shows the description of the sky in this poem? **Circle one**.

a)   b)   c)   d)

3. Which things does the narrator think are prettier? **Find** and **copy two**.

1. _____

2. _____

4. According to the narrator, where will you find a rainbow?

_____

5. Using information from the poem, put a **tick** in the correct box to show whether each statement is **true** or **false**.

	True	False
The narrator likes boats, ships and bridges.		
The narrator thinks a real bridge is better than a rainbow bridge.		
The trees reach all the way up to the clouds.		
Ships sail across the sky.		

Boats Sail on the Rivers

1. *Boats Sail on the Rivers* is also often known by the title *The Rainbow*. Write two or three sentences explaining which title you prefer and why.

_____

_____

_____

_____

2. Which statement is not a key message of this poem?

	Tick **one**
People have created some very good inventions like ships, boats and bridges.	
Natural things are better than manufactured things.	
Nature is very beautiful.	
Manufactured things are far better than nature.	

3. a) Look at the words at the end of each line. What do many of them have in common?

_____

b) What theme is the poet emphasising by using these words at the ends of the lines?

_____

Boats Sail on the Rivers

---

1. Does the poet prefer natural things or things made by people? Explain how you know.

The poet prefers _____. I know this because

_____

_____

---

2. a) Who might the poet think built "*a road from earth to sky*"?

_____

b) **Find** and **copy the word** that is a clue to who the poet thinks built the "*road from earth to sky*"?

_____

---

3. Put a **tick** in the correct box to show whether each of the following statements is a **fact** or **opinion**.

	Fact	Opinion
Clouds are far prettier than ships and boats.		
Boats sail on the rivers.		
Rainbows stretch overtops the trees.		
Bridges on the rivers are pretty.		

Prediction   Boats Sail on the Rivers

1. Boats are compared to clouds. Bridges are compared to rainbows.

Which thing in nature could street lights be compared to?

Explain your idea.

_____

_____

_____

_____

_____

2. If you could follow a road from earth to sky, what might you find? Be as imaginative as you like.

_____

_____

_____

_____

_____

1. a) This poem is written in two stanzas. How has it been divided?

	Tick **one**
In half – 5 lines then another 5 lines.	
6 lines then 4 lines.	
4 lines then 6 lines.	
2 lines then 8 lines	

b) Why has it been written in this way?

_____

_____

_____

2. This poem has the rhyme scheme ABCB ABDBCB (every second line rhymes). **Find** and **copy all the words** that rhyme with the word <u>these</u>.

_____

_____

Author's Use of Language

Boats Sail on the Rivers

1. *"But clouds that sail across the sky"*
What does this line suggest about how clouds move?

_____

_____

2. **Find** and **copy two** examples of alliteration in this poem.

1. _____

2. _____

3. *"But the bow that bridges heaven,"*
What does the word <u>bridges</u> tell the reader about the rainbow?

_____

_____

4. The poet wants the reader to look up. **Find** and **copy three words or phrases** that encourages this.

1. _____

2. _____

3. _____

Compare and Contrast

Boats Sail on the Rivers

1. How are boats and clouds similar?

_____

_____

2. How are bridges and rainbows different?

_____

_____

3. The poet prefers clouds and rainbows to boats and bridges. Why do you think this might be?

_____

_____

 #  My Shadow

by Robert Louis Stevenson

I have a little shadow that goes in and out with me,
And what can be the use of him is more than I can see.
He is very, very like me from the heels up to the head;
And I see him jump before me, when I jump into my bed.

The funniest thing about him is the way he likes to grow—
Not at all like proper children, which is always very slow;
For he sometimes shoots up taller like an India-rubber ball,
And he sometimes gets so little that there's none of him at all.

He hasn't got a notion of how children ought to play,
And can only make a fool of me in every sort of way.
He stays so close beside me, he's a coward you can see;
I'd think shame to stick to nursie as that shadow sticks to me!

One morning, very early, before the sun was up,
I rose and found the shining dew on every buttercup;
But my lazy little shadow, like an arrant sleepy-head,
Had stayed at home behind me and was fast asleep in bed.

1. **Find** and **copy one word** from the third stanza that means an idea.

_____

2. _"make a fool of me"_
Which words are closest in meaning to <u>make a fool of me</u>?

	Tick **one**
embarrass me	
joke with me	
make a cake with me	
play with me	

3. **Find** and **copy one word** from the third stanza that means the opposite of <u>hero</u>.

_____

4. _"He stays so close beside me, he's a coward you can see;_
I'd think shame to stick to nursie as that shadow sticks to me!"

Find and **copy one word** from these two lines that means the narrator would be embarrassed to behave the way the shadow is behaving.

_____

5. _"I'd think shame to stick to nursie as that shadow sticks to me!"_
Who is <u>nursie</u>?

	Tick **one**
The narrator's mum.	
The narrator's dog.	
The nurse at the doctor's surgery.	
The narrator's nanny / child-minder.	

6. _"But my lazy little shadow, like an arrant sleepy-head,"_
Find and **copy one word** from this line that means complete or total.

_____

Retrieval — My Shadow

1. **Circle** the correct options to complete the sentences below:

a) What goes in and out with the narrator?

friend	shadow
nursie	dog

b) What is the funniest thing about the shadow?

how quickly it grows	how it plays with a ball
how it jumps into bed	how it stays close to him

2. Using information from the text, put a **tick** in the correct box to show whether each statement is **true** or **false**.

	True	False
The shadow understands how to play with other children.		
The narrator thinks the shadow is very brave.		
The narrator wants to act just like the shadow.		
The shadow sticks close to the narrator whenever they go out together.		

3. Look at the fourth stanza.
When did the narrator get up?

_____

4. Where did the narrator think the shadow was when it didn't go out with him in the final stanza?

_____

My Shadow

1. Which of the following is the best set of themes for this poem?

	Tick **one**
playing, joking and laughing	
curiosity, surprise and experimenting	
friendship, love and caring	
falling out and fighting	

2. Below are some summaries of different parts of this poem. **Number them 1–4** to show the order in which they appear in the poem. The first one has been done for you.

The boy went out before sunrise while the shadow stayed in bed.	
The shadow gets bigger and smaller very quickly.	
The shadow is a coward and stays very close to the boy.	
The boy's shadow goes almost everywhere with him.	1

Inference My Shadow

1. Who is the narrator of this poem?

_____

2. *"He stays so close beside me"*
Why does the shadow actually stay so close to the narrator?

_____

3. *"And can only make a fool of me in every sort of way."*
Why is the narrator embarrassed by the shadow?

_____

_____

4. The narrator thinks the shadow is afraid of being alone.
Find and **copy one piece** of evidence that shows this.

_____

5. Why wasn't the shadow with the narrator when he went out early in the morning?

_____

_____

6. How old is the narrator in the poem? How do you know?

I think the narrator is _____ because _____

_____

My Shadow

1. What will happen when the narrator goes out on a cloudy day?

_____

_____

_____

_____

2. The shadow is the narrator's imaginary friend. What sorts of things would you do with an imaginary friend?

_____

_____

_____

_____

1. What is the rhyme scheme of this poem?

_____

2. Write the words from the poem to complete the pairs of rhyming words.

head	
up	
way	
slow	

Author's Use of Language | My Shadow

1. This poem is full of **personification**. The shadow is brought to life. What kind of character is the shadow?

_____

_____

2. _"And what can be the use of him is more than I can see."_
What does the phrase "more than I can see" tell you about the narrator?

_____

_____

3. **Find** and **copy two examples** of **alliteration** in this poem.

1. _____

2. _____

4. **Find** and **copy an example** of a simile.

_____

5. This poem is about the excitement of a child discovering his shadow.
Which is the best description of the mood of the poem?

	Tick **one**
sad and sorrowful	
annoyed and irritated	
joyful and innocent	
quiet and thoughtful	

Compare and Contrast   My Shadow

1. How is the way the shadow grows different from the way proper children grow?

_____

_____

2. "*For he sometimes shoots up taller like an India-rubber ball,*"
A simile is used to describe how the shadow grows.
Write two ways the shadow is similar to the ball.

1. _____

2. _____

3. How would the narrator behave differently to how the shadow behaves if he were a shadow himself?

_____

_____

_____

_____

Buckingham Palace

by A.A. Milne

They're changing guard at Buckingham Palace –
Christopher Robin went down with Alice.
Alice is marrying one of the guard.
"A soldier's life is terrible hard,"
      Says Alice.

They're changing guard at Buckingham Palace –
Christopher Robin went down with Alice.
We saw a guard in a sentry-box.
"One of the sergeants looks after their socks,"
      Says Alice.

They're changing guard at Buckingham Palace –
Christopher Robin went down with Alice.
We looked for the King, but he never came.
"Well, God take care of him, all the same,"
      Says Alice.

They're changing guard at Buckingham Palace –
Christopher Robin went down with Alice.
They've great big parties inside the grounds.
"I wouldn't be King for a hundred pounds,"
      Says Alice.

They're changing guard at Buckingham Palace –
Christopher Robin went down with Alice.
A face looked out, but it wasn't the King's.
"He's much too busy a–signing things,"
  Says Alice.

They're changing guard at Buckingham Palace –
Christopher Robin went down with Alice.
"Do you think the King knows all about me?"
"Sure to, dear, but it's time for tea,"
  Says Alice.

1. a) What is Buckingham Palace?

_____

b) Where is it located?

_____

2. What does the narrator mean by <u>changing guard</u>?

_____

3. Which image shows a sentry-box at Buckingham Palace? Circle one.

 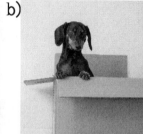  

4. _"One of the sergeants looks after their socks"_
Which word is NOT close in meaning to <u>sergeant</u>?

	Tick **one**
captain	
officer	
servant	
leader	

5. **Find** and **copy a phrase** that tells the reader where in Buckingham Palace they have great big parties.

_____

1. According to Alice, what is life like for a soldier?

_____

2. Who are Alice and Christopher Robin hoping to see?

_____

3. Why does Alice think the face they saw through the window was not the King?

_____

4. Why do Alice and Christopher Robin need to go home?

	Tick **one**
It started to rain.	
The King isn't there.	
The guard told them to leave.	
It's late in the afternoon and time for their tea.	

5. Using information from the poem, put a **tick** in the correct box to show whether each statement is **true or false**.

	True	False
Alice is marrying one of the guards.		
They spoke to the guard when they visited the palace.		
Alice was invited to a party at the palace.		
The King is very busy signing important documents.		

6. How many times do Alice and Christopher Robin go to Buckingham Palace?

_____

1. Think about the whole poem. **Which phrase** best summarises what the poem is about?

	Tick **one**
Christopher Robin doesn't like seeing the changing of the guard because they never see the King.	
Alice is going to move to Buckingham Palace after she gets married.	
Being a king is a very busy job. Some things are good and some things are difficult.	
Christopher Robin and Alice go to Buckingham Palace to talk to the King.	

Explain your choice with evidence from the text.

_____

_____

_____

_____

_____

_____

2. Below are some summaries of different parts of this text. **Number them 1–6** to show the order in which they appear in the text. The first one has been done for you.

Alice thinks the King knows all about the people he is responsible for.	
A guard was standing very smartly in his shelter.	
They never see the King because he's very busy.	
Alice wouldn't like to be king.	
Alice knows about what it's like to be a soldier because she is engaged to be married to one of them.	1
Alice and Christopher Robin were hoping to see the King.	

Inference   Buckingham Palace

1. Who might Alice be in relation to Christopher Robin (she is not his mother)? How do you know?

I think Alice is _____ because _____

_____

2. Why did Christopher Robin and Alice go to Buckingham Palace?
Give two possible reasons.

1. _____

2. _____

3. How old is Alice likely to be?

	Tick **one**
A teenager.	
A young child like Christopher Robin.	
A woman in her twenties.	
A woman older than fifty.	

4. This poem must have been written before 1952. Explain how we know this is true.

_____

_____

5. The person who looks out the window is not the King. Who might it have been?

_____

_____

6. The King is very busy. **Find** and **copy two pieces of evidence** that proves this.

1. _____

2. _____

Buckingham Palace

1. What will happen to Alice and Christopher Robin's outings to see the changing of the guard once she gets married? Why?

_____

_____

2. What sorts of things would you do if you were the King or Queen?

_____

_____

_____

_____

_____

_____

Text Meaning   Buckingham Palace

1. This poem has a very regular rhythm. How does the rhythm of the poem link to what the poem is about?

_____

_____

2. a) What is the rhyme scheme of this poem?

_____

_____

3. Write the words from the poem to complete the pairs of rhyming words.

Alice	
box	
pounds	
me	

1. Christopher Robin is the poet's son. A.A. Milne often wrote stories and poems for him. Where do we also know Christopher Robin from?

_____

2. "*Well, God take care of him, all the same,*"
What does Alice wish for the King?

_____

3. Alice understands the highs and lows of being the King.
Find and **copy one example** of each.

High	
Low	

4. The poet uses repetition to reinforce the meaning of the poem.
Find and **copy one line** that is repeated.

_____

5. **Find** and **copy two examples** of alliteration in this poem.

1. _____

2. _____

6. In other parts of the world, the changing of the guard at Buckingham Palace is often considered a symbol of Britain. Many tourists like to go to see it.
What does it represent?

_____

1. What does Christopher Robin say that makes the King seem similar to God?

_____

_____

2. How are the King and the guards similar?

_____

_____

3. How are the King and the guards different?

_____

_____

_____

_____

_____

_____

The Owl and the Pussy-Cat

by Edward Lear

The Owl and the Pussy-Cat went to sea
  In a beautiful pea-green boat.
They took some honey, and plenty of money
  Wrapped up in a five-pound note.
The Owl looked up to the stars above,
  And sang to a small guitar,
'O lovely Pussy! O Pussy, my love,
  What a beautiful Pussy you are,
    You are,
    You are!
What a beautiful Pussy you are!'

Pussy said to the Owl, 'You elegant fowl!
　　How charmingly sweet you sing!
O let us be married! too long we have tarried:
　　But what shall we do for a ring?'
They sailed away, for a year and a day,
　　To the land where the Bong-Tree grows
And there in a wood a Piggy-wig stood,
　　With a ring at the end of his nose,
　　　　His nose,
　　　　His nose!
　　With a ring at the end of his nose.

'Dear Pig, are you willing to sell for one shilling
   Your ring?' Said the Piggy, 'I will.'
So they took it away, and were married next day
   By the Turkey who lives on the hill.
They dined on mince, and slices of quince,
   Which they ate with a runcible spoon;
And hand in hand, on the edge of the sand
   They danced by the light of the moon,
      The moon,
      The moon,
They danced by the light of the moon.

Vocabulary   The Owl and the Pussy-Cat

1. In the second stanza, **find** and **copy two words** that mean bird.

_____   _____

2. "*O let us be married! too long we have tarried:*"
Which word is closest in meaning to <u>tarried</u>?

	Tick **one**
rushed	
waited	
dated	
sung	

3. In the third stanza, **find** and **copy one word** that is a type of money.

_____

4. In the third stanza, the Owl and the Pussy-Cat eat a type of fruit. What is it called?

_____

5. "*Which they ate with a runcible spoon;*"
The poet, Edward Lear, invented the word <u>runcible</u> for this poem.
Although many different people have an idea of what a "runcible spoon" might be, there is not one clear definition. **Draw a picture** of what you think it might look like in the box below.

Circle the correct answer for each question:

1. What was the Owl doing as he sang?

rowing the boat	playing piano	playing guitar	holding the money

2. Who asked the other to marry them?

The Owl asked the Pussy-Cat	The Turkey asked the Pussy-Cat	The Pig asked the Owl	The Pussy-Cat asked the Owl

3. What do they wonder in the second stanza?

What shall we do for a ring?	Where shall we go?	What shall we eat?	Do we have enough money?

4. How long did it take for them to sail to the land where the Bong-Tree grows?

a month and a day	a year and a month	a day	a year and a day

5. Where did they find the Piggy-wig?

on the sea	on the beach	in the boat	in a wood

6. Who performed the wedding ceremony?

the Turkey	the Owl	the Pussy-Cat	the Piggy-wig

7. *"And there in a wood a Piggy-wig stood,   With a ring at the end of his nose,"*
Which picture best shows the pig in this poem? **Circle one**.

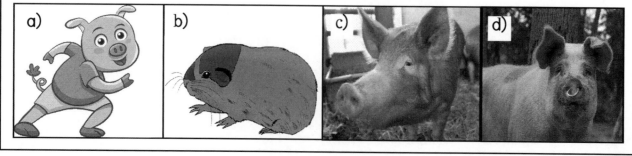

a)   b)   c)   d)

The Owl and the Pussy-Cat

1. Which of the following is a group of themes for this poem? **Circle one group**.

Love Joy Marriage	Sadness Running Away Loss
Friendship Kindness Family	Nature Spring Animals

2. Below are summaries of sections of this poem. **Number them 1–6** to show the order in which they appear in the text. The first one has been done for you.

They had a party on the beach.	
They didn't have a wedding ring.	
They decided to get married.	
They found a pig who had a ring.	
The Owl and the Pussy-Cat went to sea in a boat.	1
They were married by a turkey.	

3. *The Owl and the Pussy-Cat* is a very simple title. Which of the options below is the best choice for another possible title for this poem?

	Tick **one**
Running Away	
The Piggy-wig and the Turkey	
Journey to Happiness	
Dancing on the Beach	

Inference   The Owl and the Pussy-Cat

1. Were the Owl and the Pussy-Cat prepared for their journey? How do you know?

_____

_____

2. Why did the Owl sing to the Pussy-Cat?

_____

3. Do you think the Owl and the Pussy-Cat have known each other for a long time? **Tick one.**

yes	
no	

Why? _____

4. Was the land where the Bong-Tree grows near to their home or far away? How do you know?

I think the land where the Bong-Tree grows is _____ because

_____

5. Why did the Owl and the Pussy-Cat want to buy the Piggy-wig's ring?

_____

_____

6. Look at the third stanza. What time of day was it when they celebrated their wedding? How do you know?

It was _____ because it says _____

_____

Prediction   The Owl and the Pussy-Cat

1. What do you think the Owl and the Pussy-Cat will do next? Explain why you think this.

_____

_____

_____

_____

_____

2. Which other animal might they meet on their journey and what might that animal be doing? Think about the kinds of things the other animals are doing in this poem.

I think they will meet a _____ and it will be

_____

_____

The Owl and the Pussy-Cat

1. What is the rhyme scheme of this poem?

stanza one: _____

stanza two & three: _____

2. Look at lines 5 and 7 in each stanza. How are stanza two and three different from stanza one?

_____

_____

3. The poet uses a number of internal rhymes in this poem.
Find and **copy two examples** of an internal rhyme.

1. _____

2. _____

4. This poem is a well-known nonsense poem. Why do you think poets write nonsense poems?

_____

_____

5. How are the final four lines of each stanza like a song?

_____

_____

Author's Use of Language

The Owl and the Pussy-Cat

1. **Alliteration** is a common poetic technique. **Find** and **copy one example** of alliteration in the first stanza.

_____

2. *"Pussy said to the Owl, 'You elegant fowl!'"*
What does the word <u>elegant</u> tell us about the Owl?

_____

3. This poem is set in a fantasy land.
Find and **copy one word** from the second stanza that shows this.

_____

4. *"And hand in hand, on the edge of the sand"*
What does this phrase tell you about where the Owl and the Pussy-Cat had their wedding celebration?

_____

5. The poet uses personification to describe the animals in this poem.
Give three ways he does this.

1. _____

2. _____

3. _____

6. One of the themes of this poem is love. How does the poet show how the Owl and the Pussy-Cat feel about each other?

1. _____

2. _____

3. _____

Compare and Contrast

The Owl and the Pussy-Cat

1. a) How are the Owl and the Pussy-Cat similar?

_____

_____

b) How are the Owl and the Pussy-Cat different?

_____

_____

2. This is a <u>nonsense poem</u>. How is it different from what could happen in real life?

_____

_____

_____

_____

A Visit from St. Nicholas

by Clement Clarke Moore

Twas the night before Christmas, when all through the house
Not a creature was stirring, not even a mouse;
The stockings were hung by the chimney with care,
In hopes that St. Nicholas soon would be there;

The children were nestled all snug in their beds,
While visions of sugar-plums danced in their heads;
And mamma in her kerchief, and I in my cap,
Had just settled our brains for a long winter's nap;

When out on the lawn there rose such a clatter,
I sprang from my bed to see what was the matter,
Away to the window I flew like a flash,
Tore open the shutters and threw up the sash.

The moon, on the breast of the new-fallen snow,
Gave a lustre of mid-day to objects below;
When, what to my wondering eyes should appear,
But a miniature sleigh, and eight tiny rein-deer,

With a little old driver, so lively and quick,
I knew in a moment it must be St. Nick.
More rapid than eagles his coursers they came,
And he whistled, and shouted, and called them by name;

"Now, Dasher! now, Dancer! now, Prancer and Vixen!
On, Comet! on, Cupid! on, Dunder and Blitzen!
To the top of the porch, to the top of the wall!
Now, dash away! dash away! dash away all!"

As dry leaves that before the wild hurricane fly,
When they meet with an obstacle, mount to the sky,
So, up to the house-top the coursers they flew,
With a sleigh full of Toys, and St. Nicholas too.

And then, in a twinkling, I heard on the roof,
The prancing and pawing of each little hoof—
As I drew in my head, and was turning around,
Down the chimney St. Nicholas came with a bound.

He was dressed all in fur from his head to his foot,
And his clothes were all tarnished with ashes and soot;
A bundle of Toys he had flung on his back,
And he look'd like a peddler just opening his pack;

His eyes—how they twinkled! his dimples how merry!
His cheeks were like roses, his nose like a cherry;
His droll little mouth was drawn up like a bow,
And the beard on his chin was as white as the snow;

The stump of a pipe he held tight in his teeth,
And the smoke, it encircled his head like a wreath.
He had a broad face, and a little round belly,
That shook when he laughed, like a bowl full of jelly.

He was chubby and plump, a right jolly old elf;
And I laughed when I saw him in spite of myself;
A wink of his eye, and a twist of his head,
Soon gave me to know I had nothing to dread.

He spoke not a word, but went straight to his work,
And filled all the stockings; then turned with a jerk,
And laying his finger aside of his nose,
And giving a nod, up the chimney he rose.

He sprang to his sleigh, to his team gave a whistle,
And away they all flew like the down of a thistle;
But I heard him exclaim, ere he drove out of sight,
"Merry Christmas to all, and to all a good night!"

Vocabulary   A Visit from St. Nicholas

1. *"The children were nestled all snug in their beds,"*
Which word is closest in meaning to <u>nestled</u>?

	Tick **one**
lying	
burrowed	
sitting	
jumping	

2. In the second stanza, **find** and **copy one word** that is closest in meaning to dreams.

_____

3. *"When out on the lawn there arose such a clatter"*
What does <u>arose such a clatter</u> mean in this line?

_____

4. Look at the fourth stanza. **Find** and **copy one word** that means a shining light.

_____

5. Look at the fourth stanza. **Find** and **copy a pair** of synonyms.

_____   _____

6. *"More rapid than eagles his coursers they came,"*
<u>Coursers</u> is an unusual word. (It means ones who race or run.) What do you think it refers to?

_____

7. Look at the ninth stanza.
Find and **copy one word** that refers to a person who sells in the street or door to door.

_____

A Visit from St. Nicholas

1. When does this story take place?

_____

_____

2. Which image best describes the couple in this poem? **Circle one**.

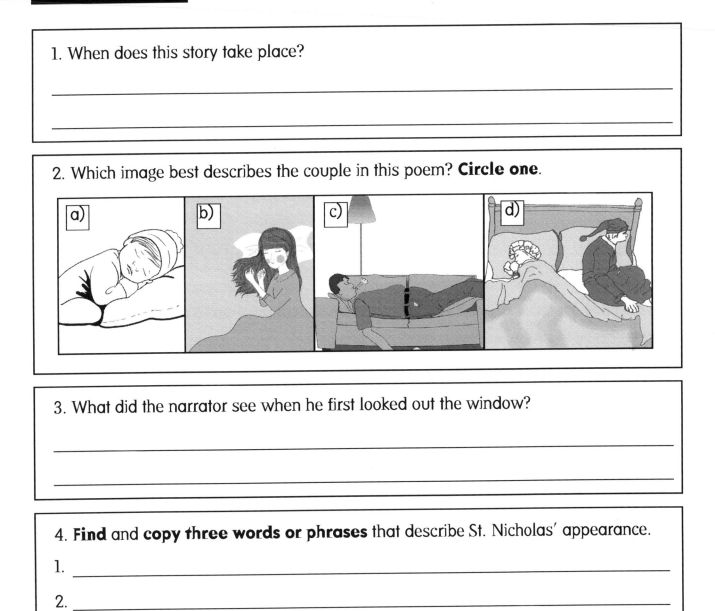

3. What did the narrator see when he first looked out the window?

_____

_____

4. **Find** and **copy three words or phrases** that describe St. Nicholas' appearance.

1. _____

2. _____

3. _____

5. How did St. Nicholas reassure the narrator that he didn't have anything to worry about? **Circle one**

| nod | wave | wink | laugh |

6. How did St. Nicolas get back up the chimney?

_____

_____

Summary   A Visit from St. Nicholas

1. Below are some summaries of different parts of this poem. **Number them 1–6** to show the order in which they appear in the text. The first one has been done for you.

Dad heard a loud noise outside the window.	
St. Nicholas filled all the stockings with toys from his sack.	
St. Nicholas came down the chimney.	
St. Nicholas went back up the chimney and flew away.	
Mum and Dad were getting ready for bed.	1
Dad looked outside and saw reindeer pulling a sleigh in the moonlight.	

2. This poem is entitled *A Visit from St. Nicholas*. It is sometimes also known as *The Night Before Christmas*.

Which would be another good title for this poem?

	Tick **one**
Christmas Dreams	
Rudolph and the Reindeer	
A Christmas Surprise	

Inference — A Visit from St. Nicholas

1. Who is the narrator of this poem? How do you know?

I know the narrator is _____ because _____

_____

2. **Find** and **copy three pieces of evidence** that tell the reader the narrator was alarmed at what was going on at the beginning of the poem.

1. _____

2. _____

3. _____

3. *"When, what to my wondering eyes should appear,"*
What is the narrator wondering about? Write your answer as a question he might be asking.

_____

_____

4. This poem is set in the Victorian time period (1800s).
Find and **copy three pieces of evidence** that it is set in the past.

1. _____

2. _____

3. _____

5. Did St. Nicholas and his reindeer move quickly or slowly? How do you know?

I know they moved _____ because _____

_____

6. St. Nicholas is shown as a very pleasant person. **Find** and **copy two pieces of evidence** that prove this.

1. _____

2. _____

A Visit from St. Nicholas

1. What will the narrator do next?

	Tick **one**
Go back to bed.	
Wake everyone up and tell them what happened.	

Explain your choice.

_____

_____

_____

_____

2. What would you do if you heard St. Nicholas on your rooftop?

_____

_____

_____

_____

Text Meaning   A Visit from St. Nicholas

1. a) What is the rhyme scheme of this poem?

_____

b) What is the impact of this rhyme scheme? What does it do for the reader?

_____

2. This is a classic Christmas poem that was first published in 1823. Many people like to repeat the final line. Why do you think the poem is still so well-known?

_____

_____

_____

_____

Author's Use of Language — A Visit from St. Nicholas

1. *"While visions of sugar-plums danced in their heads;"*
What sorts of things might the sugar-plums represent?

_____

2. *"Had just settled our brains for a long winter's nap—"*
Why is the narrator's sleep called <u>a long winter's nap</u>?

_____

3. a) Look at the third stanza. **Find** and **copy a simile** that describes how the narrator got out of bed.

_____

b) What does this simile tell us about how he moved?

_____

4. *"The moon, on the breast of the new-fallen snow,"*
What image does this phrase create of the snow in the garden?

_____

5. *"As dry leaves that before the wild hurricane fly,*
When they meet with an obstacle, mount to the sky,"
a) Which language technique is the poet using with the word "As"?

_____

b) What does it tell us about how the sleigh moves?

_____

6. *"— a right jolly old elf;"*
What does this phrase tell us about St. Nicholas?

_____

Compare and Contrast   A Visit from St. Nicholas

1. a) Look at the fifth stanza. To what other animal are the reindeer compared?

_____

b) Why is this a good comparison?

_____

_____

2. In the ninth stanza, St. Nicholas is compared to a peddler.
a) How are St. Nicholas and a peddler similar?

_____

b) How are St. Nicholas and a peddler different?

_____

3. The poet uses a lot of similes to build up a picture of St. Nicholas for his readers.
Draw lines to match each simile with its comparison.

like a wreath	St. Nicholas' belly
like a bowlful of jelly	St. Nicholas' beard
as white as the snow	St. Nicholas' mouth
like a cherry	St. Nicholas' nose
like a bow	The smoke from the pipe

4. "And away they all flew like the down of a thistle;"
How does the sleigh move through the sky as St. Nicholas leaves the house?

_____

_____

 The Eagle

by Alfred, Lord Tennyson

He clasps the crag with crooked hands;
Close to the sun in lonely lands,
Ringed with the azure world, he stands.

The wrinkled sea beneath him crawls;
He watches from his mountain walls,
And like a thunderbolt he falls.

The Eagle

1. **Find** and **copy one word** that is closest in meaning to <u>cliff</u>.

_____

2. **Find** and **copy one word** that is closest in meaning to <u>gnarled</u>.

_____

3. "*Ringed with the azure world, he stands.*"
Which phrase is closest in meaning to "<u>azure</u>"?

	Tick **one**
dark red	
bright blue	
sunny yellow	
fresh green	

4. Look at the first verse.
Find and **copy one word** that shows the eagle had to hold on tightly.

_____

5. **Find** and **copy one word** that shows the sea was moving slowly.

_____

Retrieval   The Eagle

1. What is the eagle doing on the mountain top?

_____

2. What lies beneath the eagle?

_____

3. Decide whether the following statements are **true or false**.

	True	False
The mountains are rocky.		
It is a stormy day.		
There are many birds on the mountain top.		
The eagle descends slowly from the mountain top.		

4. To whom does the mountain belong?

_____

5. What happens at the end of the poem?

	Tick **one**
The eagle flies off across the sky.	
He is joined by another eagle.	
The eagle dives down to catch some prey.	
The eagle swoops past the mountain.	

The Eagle

1. Why is the title of this poem so important?

_____

_____

2. Apart from the title, what clues are there in the text that this poem is about an eagle?

_____

_____

3. Which of the following could be an alternative title for the poem?

	Tick **one**
On Top of the World	
The Hunt	
Into the Grey Sky	
Togetherness	

Inference   The Eagle

1. *"He clasps the crag with crooked hands."*
Why does the eagle need to <u>clasp</u> the crag?

_____

_____

2. Throughout this poem, the author paints a picture of a solitary eagle. **Give two reasons** why the reader might think the eagle is isolated.

1. _____

2. _____

3. What are two ways the reader knows the mountain is very tall.

1. _____

2. _____

4. What impression is given of the sea?

1. _____

2. _____

5. *"He watches from his mountain walls,"*
What is the eagle watching for?

_____

_____

1. What do you expect to happen next? Use evidence from the poem to support your answer.

_____

_____

_____

_____

_____

_____

Text Meaning   The Eagle

1. What is the rhyme scheme of this poem?

	Tick **one**
ABABAB	
AAABBB	
ABCABC	
AABBCC	

2. Draw lines to match each poetic technique with the correct quotation from the text.

| hyperbole | And like a thunderbolt he falls. |

| alliteration | He clasps the crag with crooked hands. |

| rhyme | The wrinkled sea beneath him crawls; He watches from his mountain walls, |

| simile | Close to the sun |

Author's Use of Language   The Eagle

1. **Find** and **copy two examples** of alliteration in this poem.

1. _____

2. _____

2. *"He clasps the crag with crooked hands;"*
"...he stands."
The poet uses personification to describe the eagle. How does this technique change the reader's opinion of the eagle?

_____

_____

3. *"Ringed with the azure world, he stands."*
What does this description suggest about the scene in the poem?

_____

_____

4. *"And like a thunderbolt he falls."*
What does the simile of the <u>thunderbolt</u> suggest about the eagle?

_____

_____

5. An eagle is usually used as a symbol of freedom and bravery. How does this match with the images created in this poem?

_____

_____

_____

_____

Compare and Contrast   The Eagle

1. How is the eagle different to humans in this poem?

_____

_____

2. In the final line of the poem, the word <u>thunderbolt</u> is used to make the eagle seem god-like. Explain how.

_____

_____

The Bronze Legacy

by Effie Lee Newsome

To a Brown Boy

'Tis a noble gift to be brown, all brown,
    Like the strongest things that make up this earth,
Like the mountains grave and grand,
    Even like the very land,
    Even like the trunks of trees—
    Even oaks, to be like these!
God builds His strength in bronze.

To be brown like thrush and lark!
    Like the subtle wren so dark!
Nay, the king of beasts wears brown;
    Eagles are of this same hue.
I thank God, then, I am brown.
    Brown has mighty things to do.

Vocabulary   The Bronze Legacy

1. *"'Tis a noble gift to be brown, all brown,"*
Which word is closest in meaning to <u>noble</u>?

	Tick **one**
magnificent	
proud	
ordinary	
unimportant	

2. Look at the first stanza. **Find** and **copy one word** that is closest in meaning to <u>serious</u>.

_____

3. The thrush, lark and wren are all types of:

	Tick **one**
insects	
flowers	
birds	
lions	

4. *"Like the subtle wren so dark!"*
What does <u>subtle</u> mean in this line?

_____

_____

5. Look at the second stanza. **Find** and **copy one word** that means the same as <u>colour</u>.

_____

6. *"Brown has mighty things to do."*
Think of **two words** that could replace <u>mighty</u> in this line.

_____ _____

1. Look at the first stanza. **Find** and **copy four things** that are brown.

1. _____

2. _____

3. _____

4. _____

2. Things that are brown are the _____ things that make up this earth.

	Tick **one**
weakest	
dullest	
brightest	
strongest	

3. Look at the second stanza. **Find** and **copy four birds** that are brown.

1. _____

2. _____

3. _____

4. _____

4. Who wears brown?

_____

5. Who does the narrator say made all of these brown things?

_____

The Bronze Legacy

---

1. Why is the title of this poem so important?

	Tick **one**
It tells the reader that being brown/bronze is a wonderful gift handed down from people who came before.	
It tells the reader that the brown boy won a bronze medal at the Olympics.	
It is about people's legs.	

---

2. Each stanza ends with a strong summary statement. **Find** and **copy** these **two statements.**

stanza one:

_____

stanza two:

_____

---

3. One of the big ideas in this poem is that everyone should celebrate their own beauty and skin colour. Do you agree with this? Explain with reference to the poem.

_____

_____

_____

---

4. This poem was first published in 1922. Why is its message still important now?

_____

_____

_____

Inference The Bronze Legacy

1. a) How does the narrator feel about having brown skin? How do you know?

The narrator feels _____

I know this because it says

_____

b) Why does the narrator feel this way?

_____

_____

2. This poem is written for a brown boy. How will the brown boy feel after reading this poem?

He will feel _____ because _____

_____

3. Although this poem is written <u>To a Brown Boy</u>, people of all skin colours will read it. How will it help people who do not have brown skin? Use words from the poem to help you answer this question.

_____

_____

_____

_____

4. Which words best describe the attitude of the narrator of this poem?

	Tick **one**
content and quiet	
positive and proud	
angry and dark	
sad and lonely	

The Bronze Legacy

1. What mighty things might you do in your life?

_____

_____

_____

_____

_____

_____

2. How can you encourage other people to do mighty things?

_____

_____

_____

_____

_____

_____

_____

_____

1. Write the words from the poem to complete the pairs of rhyming words.

grand	
trees	
lark	
hue	

2. This poem has a strong rhythm. How many syllables are each of lines 3–6 and 8–13?

_____

3. The rhythm of this poem emphasises the final word in each line, telling the reader what is most important or has value. What do these emphasised words have in common?

_____

_____

1. "*'Tis a noble gift to be brown, all brown,*"
What does the word <u>gift</u> suggest about how the narrator feels about her skin colour?

_____

_____

2. "*Even oaks, to be like these!*"
What does the inclusion of an oak tree tell the reader about things and people that are brown?

_____

_____

3. Look at the first stanza. Why does the poet repeat the word "Even"?

_____

4. "*Nay, the king of beasts wears brown;*"
a) Who is <u>the king of beasts</u>?

_____

b) Where does it wear brown?

_____

5. What does the inclusion of a lion and an eagle say about being brown?

_____

_____

6. **Find** and **copy three words or phrases** that help to create a positive mood in this poem.

1. _____

2. _____

3. _____

Compare and Contrast   The Bronze Legacy

1. The poet identifies strong, natural and mighty things that are brown, like mountains, oak trees, lark, king of beasts and eagles. What is this saying about people who have brown skin?

_____

_____

2. a) In the second stanza, the poet describes a wren and an eagle. How are they different?

_____

_____

b) What does this difference tell the reader about being brown?

_____

_____

Something Told the Wild Geese

by Rachel Field

Something told the wild geese
It was time to go.
Though the fields lay golden
Something whispered, – 'Snow.'

Leaves were green and stirring,
Berries, luster–glossed,
But beneath warm feathers
Something cautioned, – 'Frost.'

All the sagging orchards
Steamed with amber spice,
But each wild breast stiffened
At remembered ice.

Something told the wild geese
It was time to fly –
Summer sun was on their wings,

Winter in their cry.

1. Look at the first stanza.
Find and **copy one word** that is opposite in meaning to <u>shouted</u>.

_____

2. _"Leaves were green and stirring,"_
Which word could replace <u>stirring</u> in this line?

	Tick **one**
cooking	
growing	
moving	
falling	

3. _"Berries, luster-glossed,"_
Explain what <u>luster-glossed</u> might mean in this sentence.

_____

4. Look at the second stanza.
Find and **copy one word** that means the same as <u>warned</u>.

_____

5. Which word describes the sound made by the geese?

	Tick **one**
told	
whispered	
cautioned	
cry	

1. At the beginning of the poem, what were the wild geese told to do?

_____

2. Which picture best shows what is happening in this poem? **Circle one**.

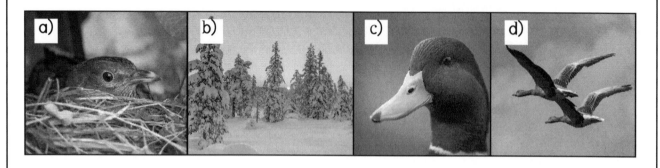

3. This poem uses many senses.
Find and **copy a word or phrase** that is an example of each sense.

sight	
sound	
smell	
touch	

4. At the end of the poem, what is it time for the wild geese to do?

_____

5. **Find** and **copy three elements** of nature described in the poem.

1. _____

2. _____

3. _____

6. What will the coming weather be like?

_____

Something Told the Wild Geese

1. Using information from the poem, tick one box in each row to show whether each summary statement is **true** or **false**.

	True	False
Wild geese know when it is time to migrate instinctively.		
Wild geese wait until the snow starts before they fly south.		
It was still warm when the geese began their journey.		
The trees and plants of the forest were bare and cold.		

2. Is *Something Told the Wild Geese* a good title for this poem? Give reasons for your answer.

	Tick **one**
yes	
no	

_____

_____

3. Suggest a different title for this poem.

_____

Something Told the Wild Geese

Keep in mind that this poem is set in northern United States of America.

1. What time of year is it? How do you know?

I know it is _____ because _____

_____

2. What will winter be like where this poem is set? How do you know?

The winter will be _____ because it says _____

_____

3. Have the geese experienced ice before? How do you know?

_____ because _____

_____

4. Why do the animals *"stiffen at remembered ice"*?

_____

_____

5. Why are the geese reacting to the changing weather?

_____

_____

6. Who or what is telling the wild geese that the snow and frost is coming?

_____

Something Told the Wild Geese

1. What are the wild geese going to do? Will they listen to the warning?
Use evidence from the poem to support your prediction.

_____

_____

_____

_____

_____

_____

2. Imagine you are a wild goose. How will it feel to fly?

_____

_____

_____

_____

_____

_____

Something Told the Wild Geese

1. What is the rhyme scheme of this poem. **Tick one**.

ABBA		ABCD	
ABCB		ABAB	

2. a) The rhythm of this poem is very consistent. What is the pattern of syllables in each stanza? **Tick one**.

5-5-5-5		6-5-6-5	
5-6-7-8		7-8-7-8	

b) Think about what this poem is about. What does this consistent rhythm remind you of?

_____

_____

Something Told the Wild Geese

1. The word <u>Something</u> is repeated four times in this poem. What sort of feeling or mood does this repetition create for the reader?

_____

2. _"Something told the wild geese"_
What does the phrase <u>wild geese</u> tell the reader about these animals?

_____

_____

3. In stanza one and two, there are three words used for personification.
Find and **copy one** of these words.

_____

4. a) Look at the final word in stanza one, two and three. How are they connected?

_____

b) What impact does this have on the reader? (What does it make the reader think?)

_____

_____

5. _"All the sagging orchards"_
What does the word <u>sagging</u> tell the reader about the orchard?

_____

_____

6. _"Summer sun was on their wings,_
   Winter in their cry."
The poet, Rachel Field, uses alliteration to create an image of the geese.
Find and **copy one example** of alliteration found in the final two lines of the poem.

_____

Compare and Contrast

Something Told the Wild Geese

1. How is the weather changing in this poem?

_____

_____

2. In the second stanza, how are the feathers different from the weather that is coming?

_____

_____

3. Do you know of any other animals which migrate in the autumn like these geese do?

Name them below.

_____

_____

_____

_____

A Bird, Came Down the Walk

by Emily Dickinson

A Bird, came down the Walk –
He did not know I saw –
He bit an Angle Worm in halves
And ate the fellow, raw,

And then he drank a Dew
From a convenient Grass –
And then hopped sidewise to the Wall
To let a Beetle pass –

He glanced with rapid eyes,
That hurried all around –
They looked like frightened Beads, I thought –
He stirred his Velvet Head

Like one in danger, Cautious,
I offered him a Crumb,
And he unrolled his feathers,
And rowed him softer home –

Than Oars divide the Ocean,
Too silver for a seam –
Or Butterflies, off Banks of Noon,
Leap, splashless as they swim.

Vocabulary   A Bird, Came Down the Walk

1. **Find** and **copy one word** from the first stanza that could be replaced with the word <u>uncooked</u>.

_____

2. _"And then he drank a Dew"_
Which is the correct definition of <u>Dew</u>?

	Tick **one**
Rain water on the grass.	
Snow melted on the ground.	
Water that evaporates from puddles.	
Water that condenses on cool surfaces overnight.	

3. Which word is closest in meaning to <u>convenient</u>?

	Tick **one**
nearby	
tall	
wet	
distant	

4. **Find** and **copy one word** from the third stanza that means <u>moving quickly</u>.

_____

5. _"He glanced with rapid eyes, / That hurried all around —"_
What does the phrase <u>all around</u> tell the reader about where the bird was looking?

	Tick **one**
It was looking everywhere.	
It was looking right in front of it.	
It was looking behind.	
It was looking up into the sky.	

6. **Find** and **copy one word** from the fourth stanza that is a synonym for careful.

_____

1. Using information from the text, put a **tick** in the correct box to show whether each statement is **true or false**.

	True	False
In the first stanza, the bird knew it was being watched.		
The bird ate seeds and berries.		
The worm was raw when the bird ate it.		
The bird drank from a blade of grass.		

2. Which other creature does the narrator see on the Walk?

_____

3. **Choose** the correct word from the options in the boxes below to complete the following sentences.

a) Flying is compared to _____ .

walking	running
rowing	hopping

b) The bird's flight is also compared to _____ .

worms	beetles
beads	butterflies

 A Bird, Came Down the Walk

1. Which of the following statements are themes for this poem?

	Tick **two**
Nature's Beauty	
Friendship with Animals	
Wonder at Nature	
Nature in Danger	

2. Below are some summaries of different parts of this poem. **Number them 1–5** to show the order in which they appear in the poem. One has been done for you.

Life is simple. The bird moves from one need to the next.	
The bird is always anxious, keeping an eye on the whole world.	
Flight is graceful like rowing in the ocean or swimming.	5
The narrator interacts with the bird who follows its instinct to fly away.	
The narrator is happy to observe the bird and notices its instinctual actions.	

Inference — A Bird, Came Down the Walk

1. In the first stanza, why does the bird act naturally?

_____

2. In the second stanza, what evidence is there that the bird is very aware of its world and notices the small things?

_____

3. How is the bird feeling in the first three stanzas? Explain how you know.

The bird is feeling _____. I know this because _____

_____

4. Look at the third stanza.
What **evidence** is there that the narrator thinks the bird is especially beautiful and soft?

_____

5. _"And he unrolled his feathers"_
What is the bird doing when it <u>unrolled his feathers</u>?

_____

6. Put a **tick** in the correct box to show whether each of the following statements is a **fact or opinion**.

	Fact	Opinion
Birds are beautiful.		
The bird drank the dew.		
The bird hopped sideways and a beetle walked past.		
Butterflies are more graceful than birds.		

A Bird, Came Down the Walk

1. Will this bird come back to the Walk? Explain your prediction with reference to the poem.

_____

_____

_____

_____

_____

2. What would you do if you spotted a bird and wanted to watch it?

_____

_____

_____

_____

_____

A Bird, Came Down the Walk

1. This poem almost has a regular rhyme scheme. Which rhyme scheme is it closest to?

	Tick **one**
couplet – AABB	
simple 4 line - ABCB	
enclosed – ABBA	
alternate - ABAB	

2. In this poem, <u>near rhymes</u> are used to fit the rhyme scheme.
Find and **copy** the <u>**near rhyme**</u> for the following words.

abroad	
home	
seam	

3. The first three stanzas have a regular rhythm. What is the pattern of the rhythm?

Tick **one**			
7-6-7-6		8-8-10-8	
6-8-6-8		6-6-8-6	

Author's Use of Language

A Bird, Came Down the Walk

1. Look at the second stanza. How does the poet suggest the bird is polite and neighbourly?

_____

2. In this poem, the bird is presented in three different ways. Draw a straight line to match the description of the bird with the correct line from the poem.

The bird is a merciless predator.	"Leap, splashless as they swim."
The bird is a beautiful, graceful creature.	"He bit an Angle Worm in halves."
The bird is an anxious and vulnerable animal.	"He glanced with rapid eyes,"

3. a) **Find** and **copy a simile** that describes the bird's eyes.

_____

b) What does this <u>simile</u> tell the reader about the bird's eyes?

_____

4. **Find** and **copy a simile** that explains how the bird feels when on the Walk.

_____

5. *"Than Oars divide the Ocean, / Too silver for a seam -"*
"Leap, splashless as they swim."
What do the ideas of being "seamless" and "splashless" suggest about the bird's flying?

_____

_____

_____

6. The final stanza is full of alliteration that adds to the beautiful comparison of flying to being in water. **Find** and **copy one example** of alliteration in this stanza.

_____

Compare and Contrast

A Bird, Came Down the Walk

1. The poet uses a simile to describe the bird's eyes. Write another simile to describe another part of the bird's body.

_____

_____

2. In the final stanza, the poet compares flying through the air to swimming in water. How is flying like swimming?

_____

_____

3. a) Write one way birds and butterflies are similar?

_____

b) Write one way birds and butterflies are different?

_____

The Cloud-Mobile

by May Swenson

Above my face is a map
where continents form and fade.
Blue countries, made
on a white sea, are erased;
white countries are traced
on a blue sea.

It is a map that moves
faster than real
but so slow;
only my watching proves
that island has being,
or that bay.

It is a model of time;
mountains are wearing away,
coasts cracking, the ocean
spills over, then new
hills heap into view
with river-cuts of blue between them.

It is a map of change:
this is the way things are
with a stone or a star.
This is the way things go,
hard or soft,
swift or slow.

1. This poem is about maps. **Find** and **copy three words** that name things we could find on a map.

_____   _____   _____

2. **Which word** means the seven main landmasses on the world map?

_____

3. "white countries are traced / on a blue sea"
Which word could replace <u>traced</u> in this line?

	Tick **one**
drawn	
erased	
cut	
modelled	

4. Look at the third stanza. **Find** and **copy a phrase** that means <u>erosion</u>.

_____

5. Which image best shows the meaning of the title, _The Cloud-Mobile?_ **Circle one**.

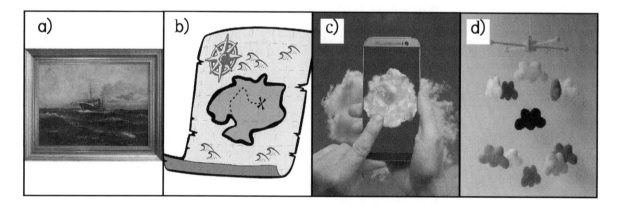

a)   b)   c)   d)

The Cloud-Mobile

1. Look at the first stanza. Where is the map?

_____

2. Look at the second stanza. What speed does the map move?

_____

3. As time passes, what is wearing away?

_____

4. What happens to the ocean?

_____

5. What cuts between the hills?

_____

6. Look at the final stanza. **Which two** things also change over time?

1. _____

2. _____

7. Using information from the text, put a **tick** in the correct box to show whether each statement is **true or false**.

	True	False
Blue countries on a white sea are erased.		
The map is not moving.		
The rivers are grey.		
The narrator is watching the clouds change.		

 The Cloud-Mobile

1. Why is the title so important in this poem?

	Tick **one**
It tells the reader the poem is about the sky.	
It is the only mention of clouds.	
It tells the reader the poem is about a map.	

2. One of the big ideas in this poem is the earth is always changing. Do you agree with this? Explain with reference to the poem.

_____

_____

_____

_____

_____

_____

Inference | The Cloud-Mobile

1. What is causing the map in the sky to move?

_____

2. How fast do real continents on the earth's surface move?

_____

3. "*only my watching proves / that island has being,*"
Why does the narrator say, <u>only my watching proves</u>?

_____

4. Which scientific cycle causes the mountains, coasts, oceans and hills of the sky and of the earth to change?

_____

5. Is the narrator surprised by the changes in the world? How do you know?

_____

_____

6. This poem focuses on the elements that shape our world.
Circle all of the elements that are included in this poem.

time	cycles	erosion
plate tectonics	change	wind

The Cloud-Mobile

1. What other shapes might you see in the clouds?

_____

_____

_____

_____

2. According to the narrator, will the world continue to change?
Use evidence from the poem to support your answer.

_____

_____

_____

_____

_____

1. Is the rhythm of this poem regular or irregular?

_____

2. Write the words from the poem to complete the pairs of rhyming words.

fade	
erased	
moves	
new	
go	

Author's Use of Language   The Cloud-Mobile

1. The title of this poem is very important. What does the phrase <u>Cloud-Mobile</u> suggest about the sky?

_____

_____

2. **Find** and **copy two examples** of alliteration in this poem.

1. _____

2. _____

3. In the first stanza, the poet uses colours to create an image. What does "*Blue countries, made on a white sea*" changing to "*white countries are traced on a blue sea*" suggest about what is happening in the sky?

_____

_____

4. "*white countries are traced / on a blue sea*"
Which part of the world could these lines symbolise?

_____

5. **Find** and **copy two words** that create an image of someone drawing the map in the sky.

_____   _____

6. **Find** and **copy four words or phrases** that show the clouds are always moving and changing.

1. _____

2. _____

3. _____

4. _____

Compare and Contrast

The Cloud-Mobile

1. a) This poem is an **extended metaphor** comparing two things. What **two things** are being compared?

_____   _____

b) Do you think this is an effective comparison? Use lines from the text to support your opinion.

_____

_____

_____

_____

2. a) Give **one way** the clouds and mountains are similar.

_____

b) Give **two ways** the clouds and mountains are different.

1. _____

2. _____

3. How do time and change work together in this poem?

_____

_____

_____

_____

The Flower-Fed Buffaloes

by Vachel Lindsay

The flower-fed buffaloes of the spring
In the days of long ago,
Ranged where the locomotives sing
And the prairie flowers lie low:—
The tossing, blooming, perfumed grass
Is swept away by the wheat,
Wheels and wheels and wheels spin by
In the spring that still is sweet.
But the flower-fed buffaloes of the spring
Left us, long ago.
They gore no more, they bellow no more,
They trundle around the hills no more:—
With the Blackfeet, lying low,
With the Pawnees, lying low,
Lying low.

Vocabulary   The Flower-Fed Buffaloes

1. This poem is about buffaloes that lived on the North American prairie.
Circle the correct picture of this type of buffalo.

a)   b)   c)   d)

2. *"Ranged where the locomotives sing"*
Which word could replace <u>locomotives</u>?

	Tick **one**
birds	
cars	
trains	
choirs	

3. *"The tossing, blooming, perfumed grass"*
Which is the correct meaning of <u>perfumed</u>?

	Tick **one**
long, tall	
emerald green	
growing	
scented	

4. **Draw lines** to match each word to the correct definition.

range		a loud, low animal cry
gore		to move in a heavy, side to side manner
bellow		to pierce with a horn or tusk
trundle		to wander and roam

Retrieval   The Flower-Fed Buffaloes

1. When did the buffalo roam the land?

_____

2. What did the buffalo eat?

_____

3. What replaced the buffalo on the prairie?

_____

4. What has replaced _"The tossing, blooming, perfumed grass"_?

_____

5. **Find** and **copy the names of two** Native American tribes who have existed since the time of the buffalo.

1. _____

2. _____

6. What is revealed at the end of the poem?

	Tick **one**
The buffalo are being brought back to the prairie.	
The Blackfeet and Pawnees have been pushed off their land too.	
Wheat grows in fields with flowers and grass.	
Locomotives are no longer on the land.	

Summary   The Flower-Fed Buffaloes

1. What is the main message of the poem?

	Tick **one**
There have been positive changes on the prairie.	
Progress has caused beautiful things of the past to vanish.	
Change is a bad thing.	
Progress and development are good.	

2. Using information from the poem, **tick** one box in each row to show whether each summary statement is **true or false**.

	True	False
The buffalo is a symbol of a vanished past.		
The poet values open spaces over urbanisation.		
The poet is excited about the development of the railway.		
The poet hopes the buffalo can come back.		

3. Think of an alternative title for this poem. Try to communicate one of the key messages of the poem in your choice.

_____

Inference   The Flower-Fed Buffaloes

1. In the first lines of the poem, what evidence is there that the buffaloes were spread over a vast region?

_____

_____

2. Think about what you know about European settlement in North America.
a) Why did the locomotive replace the buffalo?

_____

_____

b) Why did wheat replace the flowers and grass?

_____

_____

c) "*With the Blackfeet, lying low, / With the Pawnees, lying low,*"
Why are the Blackfeet and the Pawnees lying low? What does lying low mean in these lines?

_____

_____

3. In the middle of the poem, the narrator is hopeful there is still a chance that things can change back to how they used to be and the buffalo can roam the prairies again.
Find and **copy the evidence** of this in the poem.

_____

_____

The Flower-Fed Buffaloes

1. What else in nature might have vanished and been replaced in the name of progress? Explain your answer.

_____

_____

_____

_____

2. How could people have prevented the buffaloes from vanishing while still making progress with the railway and farming?

_____

_____

_____

_____

1. a) What is the rhyme scheme of the first four lines of this poem? **Tick one**.

ABBA		ABCD	
ABAC		ABAB	

b) What is the rhyme scheme of the second set of four lines (lines 5-8)? **Tick one**.

ABCB		ABCD	
ABAB		ABAC	

c) What is the rhyme scheme of the third set of four lines (lines 9-12)? **Tick one**.

AABB		ABCB	
ABAB		ABCC	

d) What do you notice about the rhyme scheme in the final three lines of the poem (lines 13-15)?

_____

e) As this poem progresses, the rhyme scheme changes and disappears. How does this link to the meaning of the poem?

_____

_____

2. Repetition is very important in this poem. What impact does the repetition of the phrases <u>no more</u> and <u>lying low</u> have on the reader? How does it make the reader feel and how does it add to the meaning of the poem?

_____

_____

_____

_____

3. Turn the poem on its side. What do you notice about the shape created by the lines?

_____

The Flower-Fed Buffaloes

1. The poet uses careful word choices to create images for the reader.
Find and **copy two words or phrases** that help to create each image below:

Image	Words or phrases that create the image.
Freedom to Move	
New Life	
Loss of Freedom	
Wind	
Sense of Smell	

2. The mood changes as the poem progresses.
a) How does the poet show a positive mood at the beginning of the poem? Use words from the poem in your answer.

_____

_____

_____

b) How does the poet show a negative change in the middle of the poem? Use words from the poem in your answer.

_____

_____

_____

c) How does the poet show a very sad and hopeless mood at the end of the poem? Use words from the poem in your answer.

_____

_____

_____

3. "*where the locomotives sing*"
What does this line suggest about the narrator's opinion of the trains?

_____

_____

_____

4. "*Wheels and wheels and wheels spin by*"
What does this line suggest about the locomotives?

_____

_____

_____

5. The poet uses alliteration to replicate the sound of the wind with the sounds **f**, **th**, **wh** and **s**.

Find and **copy two examples** of this alliteration.

1. _____

2. _____

Compare and Contrast — The Flower-Fed Buffaloes

1. *"The flower-fed buffaloes of the spring"*
What is surprising about the contrast (difference) in this line?

_____

_____

2. How are the buffaloes and the grass similar?

_____

_____

3. a) The word <u>trundle</u> could be used to describe **two things** in this poem. What are they?

_____   _____

b) How are these two things different?

_____

_____

4. How are the Blackfoot and Pawnee tribes similar to the buffaloes?

_____

_____

_____

_____

_____

_____

_____

Night

by Lucy Maud Montgomery

A pale enchanted moon is sinking low
Behind the dunes that fringe the shadowy lea,
And there is haunted starlight on the flow
Of immemorial sea.

I am alone and need no more pretend
Laughter or smile to hide a hungry heart;
I walk with solitude as with a friend
Enfolded and apart.

We tread an eerie road across the moor
Where shadows weave upon their ghostly looms,
And winds sing an old lyric that might lure
Sad queens from ancient tombs.

I am a sister to the loveliness
Of cool far hill and long-remembered shore,
Finding in it a sweet forgetfulness
Of all that hurt before.

The world of day, its bitterness and cark,
No longer have the power to make me weep;
I welcome this communion of the dark
As toilers welcome sleep.

Oh, it is well to waken with the woods
And feel, as those who wait with God alone,
The forest's heart in these rare solitudes
Beating against our own.

Close-shut behind us are the gates of care,
Divinity enfolds us, prone to bless,
And our souls kneel. Night in the wilderness
Is one great prayer.

Vocabulary Night

1. "*Behind the dunes that fringe the shadowy lea,*"
Lea means a grassland or prairie. What does this line tell you about the lea?

_____

2. "*Of immemorial sea.*"
According to this line, how old is the sea?

_____

3. Look at the second stanza. **Find** and **copy two words** that are opposite in meaning.

_____   _____

4. Look at the third stanza. **Find** and **copy one word** that is a synonym of walk.

_____

5. "*And winds sing an old lyric that might lure / Sad queens from ancient tombs.*"
According to this line, what are the winds doing to the sad queens when they lure?

_____

6. "*The world of day, its bitterness and cark,*"
The word cark is unusual. Now that it is night, all of the bad things in the day no longer have power over the narrator. What might cark mean?

_____

_____

7. Look at the final stanza. **Find** and **copy the word** that tells the reader the narrator doesn't find this solitude very often.

_____

1. The narrator is walking outdoors. **Find five words** that tell us this.

Outdoor Words	1.	2.
3.	4.	5

2. Who is the narrator with as she walks outdoors?

_____

3. What happens when the narrator goes to the "*far hill and long-remembered shore*"?

_____

_____

4. What is the daytime like for the narrator?

_____

_____

5. Look at the final stanza. What has happened to the narrator's cares?

_____

6. Which **two things** does the Divinity (God) do to those who look for solitude in the night?

_____

7. What is the narrator's soul doing at the very end of the poem?

_____

_____

 **Summary**   Night

1. Which statements are main messages of this poem?

	Tick **two**
The day is friendly.	
There is comfort in the solitude of the night.	
It is not good to be outside at night.	
Leave the troubles of the day behind.	

2. Below are summaries of sections of this poem. **Number them 1–6** to show the order in which they appear in the text. The first one has been done for you.

Shadows and wind make the night deliciously spooky.	
The moon and stars are shining on the earth below.	1
The troubles of the day have been replaced by the friendship of the dark.	
The night is familiar, like family.	
The quiet night is my friend.	
God comforts those who look for solitude in the night.	

3. The title of this poem is very simple. Write another possible title giving a little more detail. Make sure your title is no more than five words long.

_____

Inference   Night

1. "*I am alone and need no more pretend / Laughter or smile to hide a hungry heart;*"

What do these lines tell the reader about how the narrator is feeling?

_____

_____

2. Does the narrator enjoy being alone? Explain how you know.

_____

_____

3. **Find** and **copy a phrase** that is **evidence** that the narrator feels like part of the family of nature.

_____

4. Has the narrator been to the hill and shore before? How do you know?

_____

_____

5. In the fifth stanza, does the narrator still feel like crying after all the difficult things that happened during the day? Explain how you know.

_____

_____

_____

6. Look at the final stanza. How does the narrator feel connected to the forest?

_____

_____

1. How will the narrator feel about facing the challenges of the next day? Use ideas from the poem in your answer.

_____

_____

_____

_____

2. Where would you go to feel better after a difficult day? Describe why this place would make you feel better.

_____

_____

_____

_____

Night

1. a) What is the rhyme scheme of this poem?

	Tick **one**
couplet – AABB	
triplet – AAABBB	
enclosed – ABBA	
alternate - ABAB	

b) How are the final four lines of the poem different from the regular rhyme scheme?

_____

2. a) Does this poem have a regular or irregular rhythm?

_____

b) What is the pattern of the rhythm? **Tick one**.

10-6-10-6		10-10-10-6	
5-6-7-8		8-8-8-6	

c) How is the final line of the poem emphasised?

_____

3. Write words from the poem to complete the pairs of rhyming words.

sea	
heart	
looms	
weep	
care	

1. *"And there is haunted starlight on the flow / Of immemorial sea."*
What does <u>haunted starlight</u> suggest about the sea?

_____

_____

2. In the first three stanzas, the poet creates an eerie mood.
Find and **copy three words or phrases** that help to create this mood.

1. _____

2. _____

3. _____

3. **Find** and **copy two examples** of **personification** in the third stanza.

1. _____

2. _____

4. In the fourth and fifth stanzas, the mood changes. What type of mood do the following words create?

sister   **sweet**   **welcome**   **communion**

_____

5. *"I welcome this communion of the dark / As toilers welcome sleep."*
What does the poet mean by <u>communion with the dark</u>?

_____

_____

6. In the final stanza, a metaphor is used to describe "*Night in the wilderness*". To what is it being compared?

_____

Compare and Contrast   Night

1. How is the night different from the day for the narrator?

_____

_____

_____

2. "*I welcome this communion of the dark / As toilers welcome sleep.*"
How is the narrator similar to a <u>toiler</u> (someone who works hard)?

_____

_____

_____

3. Compare yourself to the narrator of this poem. Are you **similar to** or **different from** the narrator in how you feel about being outside at night? Explain.

_____

_____

_____

_____

Answers

Boats Sail on the Rivers (pages 16–24)

Boats Sail on the Rivers – Vocabulary

1. rivers / sea
2. lovelier
3. heaven
4. overtops
5. builds

Boats Sail on the Rivers – Retrieval

1. on the rivers and seas
2. answer a)

3. clouds / rainbows
4. bridging heaven / overtops the trees / from earth to sky
5.

	True	False
The narrator likes boats, ships and bridges.	x	
The narrator thinks a real bridge is better than a rainbow bridge.		x
The trees reach all the way up to the clouds.		x
Ships sail across the sky.		x

Boats Sail on the Rivers – Summary

1. Any logical, thoughtful answer that refers to the text.
2. Manufactured things are far better than nature.
3. a) Many of them are things from nature (rivers, seas, sky, trees)
   b) The beauty / importance of nature

Boats Sail on the Rivers – Inference

1. The poet prefers natural things. I know this because it says they are prettier than the things made by people.
2. a) God
   b) heaven
3.

	Fact	Opinion
Clouds are far prettier than ships and boats.		x
Boats sail on the rivers.	x	
Rainbows stretch overtops the trees.	x	
Bridges on the rivers are pretty.		x

Boats Sail on the Rivers – Prediction

1. Any logical, thoughtful answer that links to the text.

eg, Street lights could be compared to stars in the sky. They light up at night and are bright and shining. In some places there are a lot of street lights just like there are a lot of stars in the sky. Unfortunately, the light from the street lights stops us from being able to see the stars.

2. Any logical, thoughtful answer that links to the text.

Boats Sail on the Rivers – Text Meaning

1. a) 4 lines then 6 lines

   b) The first stanza (4 lines) is about the clouds and the second stanza (6 lines) is about the rainbow.

2. seas, please, trees

Boats Sail on the Rivers – Author's Use of Language

1. Sail suggests that they are blown by the wind like ships with sails. They move smoothly. The speed might change from slow to fast depending on how much wind there is. They look like they are floating in the sky.

2. And ships sail on the seas / As pretty as you please / But the bow that bridges heaven

3. It is curved / It stretches across the sky / It links two places

4. clouds / sky / heaven / overtops the trees

Boats Sail on the Rivers – Compare and Contrast

1. They are both moved by the wind. / They both move smoothly.

2. A bridge connects two pieces of land while a rainbow connects earth to sky.

A bridge goes across water however a rainbow goes across the sky.

A bridge is made of solid materials but a rainbow is made of light and water droplets.

3. Any logical, thoughtful answer that links to the text.

My Shadow (pages 25–33)

My Shadow – Vocabulary

1. notion

2. embarrass me

3. coward

4. shame

5. The narrator's nanny / child-minder

6. arrant

My Shadow – Retrieval

1. a) shadow

   b) how quickly it grows

2.

	True	False
The shadow understands how to play with other children.		x
The narrator thinks the shadow is very brave.		x
The narrator wants to act just like the shadow.		x
The shadow sticks close to the narrator whenever they go out together.	x	

3. one morning, very early, before the sun was up

4. asleep in bed

My Shadow – Summary

1. curiosity, surprise, experimenting

2.

The boy went out before sunrise while the shadow stayed in bed.	4
The shadow gets bigger and smaller very quickly.	2
The shadow is a coward and stays very close to the boy.	3
The boy's shadow goes almost everywhere with him.	1

My Shadow – Inference

1. A young boy

2. A shadow starts at a person's feet because their body is blocking the sun from their feet up to their head. This makes it look like the shadow is attached to their feet.

3. The shadow always stays close to him and looks like a coward. / It doesn't play like other children do

4. He stays so close beside me

5. The sun wasn't out yet so there were no shadows

6. I think the narrator is a young boy, maybe about 4 – 6 years old, because he goes out to play with friends but doesn't understand the science behind shadows.

My Shadow – Prediction

1. Any logical, thoughtful answer that refers to the text.

eg, The boy won't see his shadow so he might think that it has stayed home in bed or has gone away.

2. Any logical, thoughtful answer that refers to the text.

My Shadow – Text Meaning

1 AABB

2. head – bed
up – buttercup
way – play
slow – grow

My Shadow – Author's Use of Language

1. The shadow is personified as a little child.

2. He can't understand

3. heels up to the head

He stays so close beside me, he's a coward you can see

I'd think shame to stick to nursie as that shadow sticks to me

lazy little

Had stayed at home behind me and was fast asleep in bed

4. For he sometimes shoots up taller like an India-rubber ball

5. joyful and innocent

My Shadow – Compare and Contrast

1. The shadow gets larger and smaller quite suddenly while children grow taller quite gradually.

2. It goes very high

It goes up very fast

3. He would not stay so close to another person. He would be brave and do things on his own.

Buckingham Palace (pages 34–43)

Buckingham Palace – Vocabulary

1. a) The residence and offices of the reigning monarch in England. It is currently home to Queen Elizabeth II.

   b) London, England

2. The guards hand over responsibility for protecting Buckingham Palace from one set of guards to a new group. It is usually accompanied by a marching band.

3. answer a)

4. servant

5. inside the grounds

Buckingham Palace – Retrieval

1. terrible hard

2. the King

3. He's much too busy a-signing things

4. It's late in the afternoon and time for their tea.

5.

	True	False
Alice is marrying one of the guards.	x	
They spoke to the guard when they visited the palace.		x
Alice was invited to a party at the palace.		x
The King is very busy signing important documents.	x	

6. six

Buckingham Palace – Summary

1. Being a king is a very busy job. Some things are good and some things are difficult.

the King never came / I wouldn't be King for a hundred pounds / He's much too busy a-signing things / Do you think the King knows all about me? Sure to, dear

2.

Alice thinks the King knows all about the people he is responsible for.	6
A guard was standing very smartly in his shelter.	2
They never see the King because he's very busy.	5
Alice wouldn't like to be king.	4
Alice knows what it's like to be a soldier because she is engaged to be married to one of them.	1
Alice and Christopher Robin were hoping to see the King.	3

Buckingham Palace – Inference

1. sister or nanny – she is looking after Christopher Robin, she is getting married so she must be grown-up.

2. To see the guard to whom Alice is engaged.
To try to spot the King.
It's exciting to see the guards and marching band.

3. A lady in her twenties

4. A king lives at Buckingham Palace. The last king died in 1952 (Queen Elizabeth II's father, King George VI). Before Queen Elizabeth II, her father and uncle were both king – King George VI and King Edward VIII. When Queen Elizabeth II dies, there will be a king again.

5. A servant / the queen / one of the princesses

6. big parties / signing things / knows all about everyone

Buckingham Palace – Prediction

1. They will stop going together because Alice will no longer be his nanny / be able to look after him.

2. Any logical, thoughtful answer that refers to the text.

Buckingham Palace – Text Meaning

1. It sounds like the marching of the guard / the music of the marching band

2. AABBA

3. Alice – palace
   box – socks
   pounds – grounds
   me – tea

Buckingham Palace – Author's Use of Language

1. The stories about Winnie the Pooh which were also written by A.A. Milne

2. That he would be well / that God would take care of him or keep him safe

3. High – great big parties / live in a palace
Low – busy a-signing things / has to know all about everyone / very busy / no time to go out

4. They're changing guard at Buckingham Palace
Christopher Robin went down with Alice
Says Alice

5. sergeants & socks / parties & pounds / time & tea

6. the monarchy / royal family

Buckingham Palace – Compare and Contrast

1. Do you think the King knows all about me?

2. The King and the guards all work at Buckingham Palace.

3. The King works inside while the guards work outside.
The King is royal but the guards are not royal.

The Owl and the Pussy-Cat (pages 44–54)
The Owl and the Pussy-Cat – Vocabulary

1. owl / fowl

2. waited

3. shilling

4. quince

5. any drawing of a spoon-shaped object

The Owl and the Pussy-Cat – Retrieval

1. playing guitar

2. The Pussy-Cat asked the Owl

3. What shall we do for a ring?
4. a year and a day
5. in a wood
6. the Turkey
7. answer d)

The Owl and the Pussy-Cat – Summary

1. Love
   Joy
   Marriage

2.

They had a party on the beach.	6
They didn't have a wedding ring.	3
They decided to get married.	2
They found a pig who had a ring.	4
The Owl and the Pussy-Cat went to sea in a boat.	1
They were married by a turkey.	5

3. Journey to Happiness

The Owl and the Pussy-Cat – Inference

1. Yes. They had food (honey) and plenty of money.

2. To show her how much he loved her / to charm her / to woo her (make her fall in love with him)

3. Yes. They have tarried (waited) for a long time.

4. I think the land where the Bong-tree grows is far away because it took a year and a day to get there in their boat.

5. They wanted to use it as a wedding ring.

6. It was night because they danced by the light of the moon.

The Owl and the Pussy-Cat – Prediction

1. Any logical, thoughtful answer that refers to the text.

2. Any logical, thoughtful answer that links to the text.

eg, an animal doing something a human might do like a dog playing football

The Owl and the Pussy-Cat – Text Meaning

1. stanza one: ABCBDEDEEEE
stanza two & three: ABCBDEFEEEE

2. In stanza one, lines 5 and 7 rhyme with each other but in stanzas two and three, lines 5 and 7 do not rhyme with each other.

3. They took some honey, and plenty of money,
Pussy said to the Owl, "You elegant fowl!
O let us be married! too long we have tarried:

They sailed away, for a year and a day,
And there is a wood a Piggy-wig stood
Dear Pig, are you willing to sell for one shilling
So they took it away, and were married next day
They dined on mince, and slices of quince,
And hand in hand, on the edge of the sand,

4. to enjoy the sounds in the poem / for the joy or fun of the words / to enjoy the rhythm / to tell a fun story

5. The final four lines of each stanza are a chorus or a refrain like you would find in a song.

The Owl and the Pussy-Cat – Author's Use of Language

1. In a beautiful pea-green boat
And sang to a small guitar
O lovely Pussy! O Pussy, my love,

2. Elegant tells us that the Pussy-Cat thinks the Owl is graceful/handsome/dignified. The Pussy-Cat is paying the Owl a compliment and likes the Owl.

3. Bong-Tree

4. They are on a beach, near an ocean or lake

5. they talk / they sing / they play guitar / they purchase a ring / they perform a wedding ceremony / they get married / they eat with a spoon / they hold hands / they dance

6. Owl sings for the Pussy-Cat, "O lovely Pussy! O Pussy, my love, What a beautiful Pussy you are,"
They compliment each other – beautiful / elegant / How charmingly sweet you sing!
They want to get married
They hold hands
They dance with each other
They celebrate their marriage

The Owl and the Pussy-Cat – Compare and Contrast

1. a) They are both animals.
   They are both in love.
   They both want to get married and celebrate.

   b) The Owl is a bird while the Pussy-Cat is a mammal.
   The Owl is singing but the Pussy-Cat is not.
   The Pussy-Cat is described as beautiful while the Owl is described as elegant.

2. The animals sailed by themselves in a boat.
   The Owl sang and played guitar.
   The animals all spoke to each other.
   There are no real Bong-Trees.
   An Owl and a Pussy-Cat got married, celebrated and danced.

A Visit from St. Nicholas (pages 55–65)

A Visit from St. Nicholas – Vocabulary

1. burrowed

2. visions

3. there came a big noise/sound

4. lustre

5. miniature / tiny

6. the reindeer

7. peddler

A Visit from St. Nicholas – Retrieval

1. the night before Christmas / Christmas Eve

2. answer d)

3. moonlight on snow or a miniature sleigh and eight tiny reindeer

4. dressed all in fur / clothes tarnished with ashes and soot / bundle of toys on his back / like a peddler / eyes twinkled / dimples / rosy cheeks / nose like a cherry / droll (funny) little mouth like a bow / white beard / pipe / broad face / round belly / chubby and plump / jolly

5. wink

6. laying a finger aside of his nose and giving a nod

A Visit from St. Nicholas – Summary

1.

Dad heard a loud noise outside the window.	2
St. Nicholas filled all the stockings with toys from his sack.	5
St. Nicholas came down the chimney.	4
St. Nicholas went back up the chimney and flew away.	6
Mum and Dad were getting ready for bed.	1
Dad looked outside and saw reindeer pulling a sleigh in the moonlight.	3

2. A Christmas Surprise

A Visit from St. Nicholas – Inference

1. the father – it mentions children / mama / wearing a cap (night cap)

2. sprang / to see what was the matter / flew like a flash / tore / threw

3. What is making all this noise? / What is out there? / What could it be? / Am I really seeing this?

4. kerchief / cap / shutters / sash / peddler / pipe

5. quickly – dash / fly / mount / flew / bound / more rapid than eagles

6. His eyes – how they twinkled / his dimples how merry / his cheeks were like roses / his nose like a cherry / droll little mouth was drawn up like a bow / laughed / a right jolly old elf

A Visit from St. Nicholas – Prediction

1. Any logical, thoughtful answer that refers to the text.
(eg, He might wake everyone up because he was really excited about what he had seen. OR He might go back to bed because he didn't want to spoil the surprise for everyone in the morning.)

2. Any logical, thoughtful answer that refers to the text.

A Visit from St. Nicholas – Text Meaning

1. a) AABB (rhyming couplets)

   b) It helps the reader to remember the poem. / It makes the poem more enjoyable and lyrical – like a song./ It helps to give the poem a happy mood.

2. Any logical, thoughtful answer that refers to the text.

A Visit from St. Nicholas – Author's Use of Language

1. Things the children want – wishes / sweets / toys

2. It is near Christmas and the Winter Solstice so there are many hours of darkness. / Also, nap rhymes with cap so it works in the rhyme scheme of the poem.

3. a) flew like a flash

   b) He moved quickly.

4. breast – rounded / curved / snow drift
new-fallen – unbroken / smooth / no footprints

5. a) simile

   b) It moves quickly near the ground then goes straight up when it gets close to an object like a house.

6. jolly – happy / cheerful / pleasant
old – aged / ancient / been around for a long time
elf – magical / not human

A Visit from St. Nicholas – Compare and Contrast

1. a) eagles
   b) Eagles can fly very fast and St. Nicholas and the reindeer were even faster so it gives us an idea of how quickly they could move.

2. a) They both have a sack full of things people want.

   b) St. Nicholas is giving things away but/however a peddler is selling the items in his/her sack.

3 like a wreath – The smoke from the pipe
   like a bowlful of jelly – St. Nicholas' belly
   as white as the snow – St. Nicholas' beard
   like a cherry – St. Nicholas' nose
   like a bow - St. Nicholas' mouth

4. It floats lightly on the air as if it is being blown.

The Eagle (pages 66–74)
The Eagle – Vocabulary

1. crag

2. crooked

3. bright blue

4. clasps

5. crawled

The Eagle – Retrieval

1. clasping the rock / standing / watching

2. the (wrinkled) sea

3.

	True	False
The mountains are rocky.	x	
It is a stormy day.		x
There are many birds on the mountain top.		x
The eagle descends slowly from the mountain top.		x

4. The eagle

5. The eagle dives down to catch some prey.

The Eagle – Summary

1. It tells us what the poem is about. It doesn't ever say it's an eagle in the poem itself.
2. Crooked hands (talons) / up on a mountain top / diving down towards the sea
3. On Top of the World

The Eagle – Inference

1. He is very high up. He needs to hold on so he doesn't fall.
2. Lonely lands / he is high on a mountain top where most other creatures would struggle to get to
3. Close to the sun / his mountain walls
4. It is old or has been there for a long time (wrinkled) / It is moving slowly. It's a calm day so not very wavy. / It is blue (azure)
5. He is watching for prey – something he can hunt and eat.

The Eagle – Prediction

1. Any logical, thoughtful answer that refers to the text.

eg, The eagle will capture its prey after diving like a thunderbolt. Then it will return to the mountain top to continue watching the world around him.

The Eagle – Text Meaning

1. AAABBB
2. <u>hyperbole</u> – Close to the sun

    <u>alliteration</u> – He clasps the crag with crooked hands.

    <u>rhyme</u> – The wrinkled sea beneath him crawls;

            He watches from his mountain walls,

    <u>simile</u> – And like a thunderbolt he falls.

The Eagle – Author's Use of Language

1. He clasps the crag with crooked hands / lonely lands / He watches from his mountain walls
2. It makes the eagle seem more important. It makes the eagle seem human-like.
3. There is a circle of beautiful blue sky with the sea below surrounding the eagle.
4. He flies straight downward quickly and sharply like a thunderbolt shoots across the sky. / It makes the eagle seem powerful and dangerous.
5. Freedom – The eagle can go anywhere. He is able to fly to places humans cannot reach like the top of high mountains. He is on his own and able to do what ever he wants to do.

Bravery – The eagle is not afraid of being up so high or diving down quickly. It is a powerful predator who can swoop down on its prey.

The Eagle – Compare and Contrast

1. The eagle can go somewhere humans would struggle to get to.
2. The thunderbolt reminds us of the Greek god Zeus who had a thunderbolt as a weapon.

The Bronze Legacy (pages 75–83)

The Bronze Legacy – Vocabulary

1. magnificent
2. grave
3. birds
4. delicate / quiet / small / inconspicuous

5. hue

6. important / significant / big / strong / powerful / extraordinary

The Bronze Legacy – Retrieval

1. earth / mountains / land / trunks of trees / oaks

2. strongest

3. thrush / lark / wren / eagle

4. the king of beasts / a lion

5. God

The Bronze Legacy – Summary

1. It tells the reader that being brown/bronze is a wonderful gift handed down from people who came before.

2. stanza one: God builds his strength in bronze.

stanza two: Brown has mighty things to do.

3. Any logical, thoughtful answer that refers to the text.

4. Any logical, thoughtful answer that refers to the text.

The Bronze Legacy – Inference

1. a) The narrator feels proud / happy / glad /thankful

I know this because it says Tis a noble gift / God builds his strength in Bronze / I thank God that I am brown / Brown has mighty things to do.

    b) Things/people that are brown are strong / mighty / made by God / natural / connected to the earth / given a gift

2. He will feel proud / happy / thankful / encouraged / valued

because the poet is talking about how good it is to have brown skin and all of the other good things that are brown.

3. Any logical, thoughtful answer that refers to the text.

eg, It will encourage all people to value people with brown skin. It will help them to see that many things in the world are brown and they are strong and mighty. Things like mountains, trees, lions and eagles are valued. People with brown skin should be valued too.

4. positive and proud

The Bronze Legacy – Prediction

1. Any logical, thoughtful answer

2. Any logical, thoughtful answer

The Bronze Legacy – Text Meaning

1. grand – land
    trees – these
    lark – dark
    hue – do

2. 7

3. The emphasised words are either brown or things that occur in nature like earth, land, trees, lark. This shows the reader that being brown is important and natural.

The Bronze Legacy – Author's Use of Language

1. She is pleased with it / treasures it / was glad to receive it / grateful

2. Oak trees are symbols of strength. People who are brown must be strong like an oak tree.

3. She is showing there are a lot of things that are brown.

4. a) lion

    b) on its mane

Classic Poetry Years 3–4
142

© Brilliant Publications Limited

5. Lions and eagles are respected, strong, dangerous, mighty, symbols of leadership. Things that are brown, including people, are like them.

6. gift / noble / strongest / bronze / grand / strength / thank God / mighty

The Bronze Legacy – Compare and Contrast

1. By comparing people with brown skin to these other strong, natural and mighty things, the poet is saying that people with brown skin are strong, natural and mighty too.

2. a) A wren is very small while an eagle is large.
   A wren eats seeds and berries but an eagle hunts for prey.

   b) Brown things come in all shapes and sizes. They come from all parts of life. They are all important.

Something Told the Wild Geese (pages 84–92)

Something Told the Wild Geese – Vocabulary

1. whispered
2. moving
3. shiny / bright / glittery / glowing / like they'd been painted
4. cautioned
5. cry

Something Told the Wild Geese – Retrieval

1. to go
2. answer d)

3. sight – wild geese / berries / frost / snow / ice / fields / leaves / orchards
   sound – told / whispered / cautioned / cry
   smell – amber spice
   touch – warm / frost / summer sun / ice / snow
4. time to fly
5. geese / fields / snow / berries / leaves / orchards / ice / frost
6. wintery / cold / snowy / icy

Something Told the Wild Geese – Summary

1.

	True	False
Wild geese know when it is time to migrate instinctively.	x	
Wild geese wait until the snow starts before they fly south.		x
It was still warm when the geese began their journey.	x	
The trees and plants of the forest were bare and cold.		x

2. Any logical, thoughtful answer that refers to the text.

3. Any logical, thoughtful answer that refers to the text.

Something Told the Wild Geese – Inference

1. late summer or early autumn because leaves are green / orchards are sagging with fruit / geese are getting ready to migrate / winter is coming

2. It will be cold / frosty / snowy because it warns of snow, frost and ice coming / the geese have to migrate.

3. Yes because it says "each wild breast stiffened at remembered ice." They remember the feeling of ice.

4. They remembered the feeling of the cold and how it made them shiver or go rigid.

5. They have a natural instinct to fly south to warmer climates when winter is coming.

6. It is their natural instinct / nature / mother nature.

Something Told the Wild Geese – Prediction

1. Any logical, thoughtful answer that explains how the geese are going to migrate / fly south with reference to the poem.

2. Any logical, thoughtful answer.

Something Told the Wild Geese – Text Meaning

1. ABCB

2. a) 6-5-6-5

   b) The regular rhythm of the geese's wings flapping as they fly.

Something Told the Wild Geese – Author's Use of Language

1. mysterious / wondering / questioning

2. They are free. They are not controlled by people. They are large birds who fly south / migrate.

3. told / whispered / cautioned

4. a) They are all cold, wintery words.

   b) It makes the reader think that winter is coming.

5. The trees are full of fruit that is heavy and making the branches sag / bend.

6. summer sun / wings winter

Something Told the Wild Geese – Compare and Contrast

1. It is changing from warm to cold.

2. The feathers are warm but the weather is frosty / cold.

3. monarch butterfly / hummingbirds / whales / wildebeests / pronghorns / swallows / Arctic terns / sandhill crane / elephants / salmon / leatherback turtles / caribou
and many others.

A Bird, Came Down the Walk (pages 93–102)

A Bird, Came Down the Walk – Vocabulary

1. raw

2. Water that condenses on cool surfaces overnight.

3. nearby

4. rapid / hurried

5. It was looking everywhere.

6. cautious

A Bird, Came Down the Walk – Retrieval

1.

	True	False
In the first stanza, the bird knew it was being watched.		x
The bird ate seeds and berries.		x
The worm was raw when the bird ate it.	x	
The bird drank from a blade of grass.	x	

2. Angle Worm / beetle

3. a) rowing
   b) butterflies

A Bird, Came Down the Walk – Summary

1. Nature's Beauty / Wonder at Nature

2.

Life is simple. The bird moves from one need to the next.	2
The bird is always anxious, keeping an eye on the whole world.	3
Flight is graceful like rowing in the ocean or swimming.	5
The narrator interacts with the bird who follows its instinct to fly away.	4
The narrator is happy to observe the bird and notices its instinctual actions.	1

A Bird, Came Down the Walk – Inference

1. It doesn't know it is being watched.

2. It sees the dew on the grass. / It noticed the beetle and hopped out of the way to let it pass.

3. anxious / worried / scared – glanced with rapid eyes / hurried all abroad / looked like frightened Beads

4. He stirred his Velvet Head.

5. Stretching out its wings to fly away

6.

	Fact	Opinion
Birds are beautiful.		x
The bird drank the dew.	x	
The bird hopped sideways and a beetle walked past.	x	
Butterflies are more graceful than birds.		x

A Bird, Came Down the Walk – Prediction

1. Any logical, thoughtful answer that refers to the text.

2. Any logical, thoughtful answer that refers to the text.

A Bird, Came Down the Walk – Text Meaning

1. simple 4 line – ABCB

2. abroad – head
   home – crumb
   seam – swim

3. 6-6-8-6

A Bird, Came Down the Walk – Author's Use of Language

1. It hops out of the way to let the beetle pass.

2. The bird is a merciless predator – "He bit an Angle Worm in halves."
The bird is a beautiful, graceful creature – "Leap, Splashless as they swim."
The bird is an anxious and vulnerable animal – "He glanced with rapid eyes,"

3. a) like frightened Beads
    b) small, round, rolling/moving around

4. Like one in danger

5. The bird and the sky are as one / they are a part of each other.
The bird's flying is graceful and effortless. Its wings go through the air easily /effortlessly. Its movements are neat and efficient.

6. Oars divide the Ocean
    Too silver for a seam
    Butterflies off Banks of Noon
    splashless as they swim

A Bird, Came Down the Walk – Compare and Contrast

1. Any logical, thoughtful answer that refers to the text.

2. They are both smooth and graceful.
Your feet don't touch the ground.
You use fast, powerful movements.

3. a) They both fly. / They both have wings. / They are both graceful.
    b) Butterflies are insects, not birds. / Birds have feathers **but** butterflies do not. / Butterflies are very small **while** birds are usually larger.

The Cloud-Mobile (pages 103–111)

The Cloud-Mobile – Vocabulary

1. continents / countries / sea / bay / island / mountains / coasts / hills / river

2. continents

3. drawn

4. wearing away

5. answer d)

The Cloud-Mobile – Retrieval

1. Above the narrator's face / In the sky

2. So slow / Faster than the continents move in real life

3. mountains

4. It spills over

5. A river

6. stone / star

7.

	True	False
Blue countries on a white sea are erased.	x	
The map is not moving.		x
The rivers are grey.		x
The narrator is watching the clouds change.	x	

The Cloud-Mobile – Summary

1. It is the only mention of clouds.
2. Any logical, thoughtful answer that links to the text.

The Cloud-Mobile – Inference

1. wind / air currents
2. Very slowly
3. If the narrator were to look away, they wouldn't notice the clouds had moved at all. It is only through watching them carefully that movement can be seen because they are moving so slowly.
4. water cycle
5. No, it says, "this is the way things are" and "this is the way things go". The narrator knows that these changes are natural and it is what has always happened.
6. time / cycles / erosion / plate tectonics / change / wind – all 6 answers are correct

The Cloud-Mobile – Prediction

1. Any logical, thoughtful answer that links to the text.
2. Yes. In the final stanza it says, "this is the way things are" and "this is the way things go". This suggests that the changes will keep happening.

The Cloud-Mobile – Text Meaning

1. irregular
2. fade – made
   erased – traced
   moves – proves
   new – view
   go – slow

The Cloud-Mobile – Author's Use of Language

1. The clouds are hanging from the sky above the narrator like a baby's mobile above the cot. They are moving slowly.
2. form and fade / that island has being or that bay / coasts cracking / hills heap / stone or a star / swift or slow
3. At first the sky is mostly white – very cloudy. Then the sky changes to be mostly blue – the clouds have cleared and there is more blue sky with some clouds.
4. Antarctica
5. erased / traced
6. form and fade / made / erased / traced / moves / faster / slow / that island has being / cracking / spills over / heap into view / river-cuts of blue between them / map that moves / map of change

The Cloud-Mobile – Compare and Contrast

1. a) The clouds in the sky are compared to a map of the world (the continents on earth).
   b) Any logical, thoughtful answer that links to the text.

2. a) They are **both** changing / They are **both** large and jagged.
   b) The clouds are made of water vapour **but** mountains are made of rock. / The clouds are in the sky **while** real mountains are on earth.

3. The changes caused by wind, water and erosion continue over time. The more time that passes, the more change takes place.

The Flower-Fed Buffaloes (pages 112–121)

The Flower-Fed Buffaloes – Vocabulary

1. answer c)

2. trains
3. scented
4. range – to wander and roam
   gore – to pierce with a horn or tusk
   bellow – a loud, low animal cry
   trundle – to move in a heavy, side to side manner

The Flower-Fed Buffaloes – Retrieval

1. In the days of long ago
2. flowers
3. locomotives
4. wheat
5. Blackfeet (Blackfoot) / Pawnee(s)
6. The Blackfeet and Pawnees have been pushed off their land too.

The Flower-Fed Buffaloes – Summary

1. Progress has caused beautiful things of the past to vanish.
2.

	True	False
The buffalo is a symbol of the vanished past.	x	
The poet values open spaces over urbanisation.	x	
The poet is excited about the development of the railway.		x
The poet hopes the buffalo can come back.	x	

3. Any logical, thoughtful answer that refers to the text.

The Flower-Fed Buffaloes – Inference

1. They ranged where the locomotives sing which means they roamed over the area where the trains went.

2. a) European settlers wanted to travel long distances across the country. When they built the railway, they destroyed the buffalo's habitat and many buffaloes were hunted.
   b) Farming was being developed. More settlers meant more food was needed. Farmers used grassland for crops.
   c) They are lying low just like the prairie flowers. Their tribes have been pushed off their land by European settlers just like the native plants and the buffaloes.

3. The poet says, "In the spring that is still sweet". This is a line of hope in the middle of everything being pushed out by the locomotives and the farming.

The Flower-Fed Buffaloes – Prediction

1. Any logical, thoughtful answer that links to the text.

2. Any logical, thoughtful answer that refers to the text.

The Flower-Fed Buffaloes – Text Meaning

1. a) ABAB
   b) ABCB
   c) ABCC
   d) The final three lines rhyme with the repetition of the phrase "lying low".
   e) The rhyme scheme disappears just like the buffaloes disappear.

2. The repetition of these lines emphasises the loss of the buffaloes and native plants. Repetition creates a dark, sad, hopeless feeling.

3. The lines create the shape of a buffalo. Start at the bottom of the poem to see its head then a short neck, four legs and a tail.

The Flower-Fed Buffaloes – Author's Use of Language

1. Freedom to Move: ranged / prairie / tossing
New Life: flower-fed / spring / blooming
Loss of Freedom: lie low / swept away
Wind: tossing / swept away
Sense of Smell: perfumed / sweet

2. a) The beginning of the poem is full of life with the flowers, buffaloes and blooming, perfumed grass. The buffaloes are free to roam (ranged) .

   b) In the middle of the poem, the blooming, perfumed grass is swept away by the wheat. The locomotives have taken over. There are a lot of them and they cover long distances ("Wheels and wheels and wheels…"). There is still a little bit of hope with the line "In the spring that is still sweet".

   c) The repetition of the phrases "no more" and "lying low" show sadness and hopelessness. Even the people who originally lived on the land have been pushed out ("With the Blackfeet, lying low / With the Pawnees, lying low").

3. The word "sing" makes the trains sound positive. The narrator romanticises them a bit (thinks of them in an idealised way). The narrator could also be speaking sarcastically in saying they "sing" when really they make a horrible, loud noise that disturbs nature.

4. The repetition of "wheels" makes it seem like there are a lot of them and the train tracks go a long way.

5. flower-fed buffaloes of the spring / tossing, blooming, perfumed grass / Is swept away by the wheat / Wheels and wheels and wheels… / In the spring that still is sweet

The Flower-Fed Buffaloes – Compare and Contrast

1. The very large animals are eating very small flowers.

2. They have both been swept away / destroyed by progress and the coming of new things due to settlers / colonisation.

3. a) buffaloes / locomotives

   b) Buffaloes are natural, living animals while locomotives are human-made machines.

4. They have been driven off their land (swept away) by the European settlers and colonisation just like the buffalo have.

Night (pages 122–131)

Night – Vocabulary

1. It is surrounded / edged / bordered by sand dunes.

2. ancient / always been there

3. enfolded, apart

4. tread

5. call / entice / bait / tempt

6. troubles, worries, burdens

7. rare

Night – Retrieval

1. moon / dunes / lea / starlight / sea / moor / winds / hill / shore

2. She is alone

3. She forgets everything that has hurt her before.

4. The day is full of bitterness and troubles (cark). It has made her weep (cry).

5. Her cares are shut behind a gate.

6. enfolds / hugs / comforts and blesses

7. kneeling to pray

Night – Summary

1. There is comfort in the solitude of the night. / Leave the troubles of the day behind.

2.

Shadows and wind make the night deliciously spooky.	3
The moon and stars are shining on the earth below.	1
The troubles of the day have been replaced by the friendship of the dark.	5
The night is familiar, like family.	4
The quiet night is my friend.	2
God comforts those who look for solitude in the night.	6

3. Any logical, thoughtful answer that refers to the text.

Night – Inference

1. She has been laughing and smiling to hide how she really feels. There is something missing from her heart / she is longing for something.

2. Yes – I walk with solitude as with a friend.

3. I am a sister

4. Yes – long-remembered shore

5. No – No longer have the power to make me weep

6. It's like their hearts are beating together.

Night – Prediction

1. Any logical, thoughtful answer that refers to the text.

2. Any logical, thoughtful answer that links to ideas in the text.

Night – Text Meaning

1. a) alternate – ABAB

   b) The rhyme scheme changes to ABBA (or it could be called CDDC)

2. a) regular

   b) 10-10-10-6

   c) It has only 4 syllables, making it stand out.

3. sea – lea
   heart – apart
   looms – tombs
   weep – sleep
   care – prayer

Night – Author's Use of Language

1. It is shining and sparkly. The stars are reflecting in the water. It creates an eerie/spooky feeling.

2. enchanted / haunted / shadows / ghostly / ancient tombs

3. shadows weave / winds sing

4. comforting / friendly / welcoming / kind

5. friendship / closeness with the dark and the night. The narrator feels comfortable being out in the night.

6. one great prayer

Night – Compare and Contrast

1. The day is full of troubles while the night is peaceful / friendly / comfortable / refreshing.

2. They both rest at night. Someone who works hard looks forward to sleep and rest at night. In the same way, the narrator needs the night to recover from all of the difficult things that happen during the day.

3. Any logical, thoughtful answer that refers to the text.

Photograph Credits

Boats Sail on Rivers

p 16	river; Marcin Waz: Pixabay
p 18, 132	rainbow; Ykaiavu: Pixabay
p 18	Two photographs combined: Clouds; Klickblick: Pixabay and Yacht; Paul PR75: Pixabay
p 18	Beach; Jonny Belvedere: Pixabay (photoshopped and cropped)
p 18	golden gate; Constanze Zeiger: Pixabay
p 22	pont du gard; Ira Gorelick: Pixabay
p 24	rainbow; Brigichtal: Pixabay

My Shadow

| p 28 | shadow; MW: Pixabay |
| p 31 | run-jump-shadow; Manseok Kim: Pixabay |

Buckingham Palace

p 36, 135	buckingham-palace-2-Waldiwkl: Unsplash
p 36	dog in box; erda-estremera-sxNt9g77PE0: Unsplash
p 36	garden shed; Andy Watkins-HebulLtR3yA: Unsplash
p 36	london; TeeFarm: Pixabay
p 40	Crown Jewels of the United Kingdom: Wikipedia
p 41	Buckingham Palace; Waldiwkl: Pixabay
p 43	Coach and Horses; Addesia: Pixabay

The Owl and The Pussycat

p 44	The Owl and the Pussycat; Uncredited illustrator: Child life
p 45	The Owl and the Pussycat, Edward Lear: American Literature
p 46	The Owl and the Pussycat Edward Lear and Leonard Leslie Brooke; Commons Wikimedia

p 96	robin; Capri 23 Auto: Pixabay
p 98	Bird bath; Jill Wellington: Pixabay
p 101	Humming bird; Pexels: Pixabay
p 102	Peacock butterfly; Couleur: Pixabay

The Cloud-Mobile

p 104	oil painting; Steve Zhang: Pixabay
	treasure map; Open Clipart Vectors: Pixabay
	cloud; Gerd Altmann: Pixabay
p 104, 146	cloud mobile; Brilliant Publications Ltd
p 106	Road; Ryan McGuire: Pixabay
p 108	Neanderthals; David Mark: Pixabay
p 109	Sun Rays; Marco Roosink: Pixabay

The Flower-fed Buffaloes

p 112	bison; Georg Schober: Pixabay
p 113	water-buffalo; Markus Fischer: Pixabay
p 113	simmental-cattle; Stephan and Tina Forstmann: Pixabay
p 113	bull; UlrikeLeone: Pixabay
p 113, 148	bison; Wiki Images: Pixabay
p 117	buffalo; ante89: Pixabay
p 120	Steamtrain; Steve Brandon: Pixabay
p 121	When the Land Belonged to God, painting by C.M. Russell: Wikipedia

Night

p 122	Path; Free Photos
p 126	clay-banks-YFZ-kMS0nFs-unsplash
p 128	animals; Mabuya: Pixabay
p 131	teddy; Alexus Photos: Pixabay

Front cover

woman carrying child; Pieter01: Pixabay
Santa-climbing-down-the-chimney; Unknown illustrator; Commons Wikimedia
Buckingham Palace; Waldwikl: Pixabay
The Owl and the Pussycat; Uncredited illustrator, Child life: Commons Wkimedia
Bald Eagle; Public Domain Pictures
run-jump-shadow; Manseok Kim: Pixabay
Wild geese: gary-bendig-WPmPsdX2ySw-unsplash

Acknowledgements

We are grateful to the following for permission to reproduce copyright material:

The poem "The Cloud-Mobile" by May Swenson, copyright © 1958. Reproduced by kind permission of the Literary Estate for May Swenson; The poem "Buckingham Palace" by A.A. Milne from Winnie The Pooh: The Complete Collection of Stories and Poems, text copyright © The Trustees of the Pooh Properties, 2016. Reproduced by permission of HarperCollins Publishers Ltd, and Curtis Brown Ltd, London; and the poem "The Flower-Fed Buffaloes" by Vachel Lindsay, copyright © 1926. Reproduced by kind permission of the estate of Vachel Lindsay.

In some instances we have been unable to trace the owners of copyright material, and we would appreciate any information that would enable us to do so.

References

English Reading Test Framework, National curriculum tests from 2016, 2016 Key Stage 2 English Reading Test Framework: National Curriculum Tests from 2016 Electronic version product code: STA/15/7341/e ISBN: 978-1-78315-826-3

Lexico. Definition of classic in English. https://www.lexico.com/en/definition/classic

The National Curriculum in England Framework document December 2014, Reference: DFE-00177-2013

Poems:
Rosetti, Christina. "Boats Sail on the Rivers". *Sing-song: a nursery rhyme book*. London: George Routledge & Sons, 1872
Rosetti, Christina. "Boats Sail on the Rivers". Favourite Poems to Read Aloud. New York: Wonder Books, 1965.

Stevenson, Robert Louis. "My Shadow". *A Child's Garden of Verses*. London: Longmans, Green and Co., 1885.
Stevenson, Robert Louis. "My Shadow". *A Child's Garden of Verses*. New York: Charles Scribner's Sons, 1905.
(Project Gutenberg: http://www.gutenberg.org/files/25609/25609-h/25609-h.htm)

Milne, A.A. "Buckingham Palace". *When We Were Very Young*. London: Methuen & Co., 1924
Milne, A.A. "Buckingham Palace". *When We Were Very Young*. New York: Dell Publishing Co. Inc., 1980.

Lear, Edward, "The Owl and the Pussy-Cat". *Nonsense Songs, Stories, Botany, and Alphabets*. London: Robert John Bush, 1871.
Lear, Edward. "The Owl and the Pussy-Cat". *The Nation's Favourite Poems*. BBC Worldwide Ltd, 1996.

Moore, Clement Clarke. "A Visit from St Nicholas". Troy Sentinel, New York: December 23, 1823.
Moore, Clement Clarke. "A Visit from St. Nicholas" Illustrated by F.O.C. Darley. New York: James G. Gregory, 1862.
(http://www.gutenberg.org/files/17382/17382-h/17382-h.htm)

Tennyson, Alfred, Lord. "The Eagle". *Poems*. London: Edward Moxon, 1851.
Tennyson, Alfred, Lord. "The Eagle". *The Kingfisher Book of Children's Poetry*. London: Kingfisher Books Ltd, 1985.

Newsome, Effie Lee. "The Bronze Legacy". *"The Crisis"* vol. 24 no. 6, October 1922.
(https://modjourn.org/issue/bdr521702/#)

Field, Rachel. "Something Told the Wild Geese". *Branches Green*. New York: The Macmillan Company, 1934.
Field, Rachel. "Something Told the Wild Geese". *One Hundred Years of Poetry for Children*. Oxford: Oxford University Press, 1999.

Dickinson, Emily. "A Bird Came Down the Walk". *Poems Second Series*. Boston: Roberts Brothers, 1891.
Dickinson, Emily. "A Bird Came Down the Walk". *The Kingfisher Book of Children's Poetry*. London: Kingfisher Books Ltd, 1985.

Swenson, May. "The Cloud-Mobile". *A Cage of Spines*. New York: Rinehart & Company, Inc, 1958.
Swenson, May. "The Cloud-Mobile". *The Kingfisher Book of Children's Poetry*. London: Kingfisher Books Ltd, 1985.

Lindsay, Vachel. "The Flower-Fed Buffaloes". *Going-to-the-Stars*. New York: D. Appleton, 1926.
Lindsay, Vachel. "The Flower-Fed Buffaloes". *One Hundred Years of Poetry for Children*. Oxford: Oxford University Press, 1999.

Montgomery, Lucy Maud. "Night". *Canadian Magazine*. Toronto: Hugh C. Maclean Publications, Limited, Jan. 1935.
Montgomery, Lucy Maud. "Night". *Ultimate Collection: 29 Novels & 170+ Short Stories, Poetry, Letters and Autobiography*. E-Artnow, 2016.

Information about Poets and Poems

Analysis of 'The Flower-Fed Buffaloes'. *English Language Literature.* (accessed January 2021)
https://englishlanguageliterature.wordpress.com/2011/03/25/analysis-of-the-flower-fed-buffaloes/

Baldwin, Emma. Emily Dickinson: A Bird Came Down the Walk. Poem Analysis. (accessed January 2021).
https://poemanalysis.com/emily-dickinson/a-bird-came-down-the-walk/

The Flower-Fed Buffaloes. Poetry Prof. (accessed January 2021)
https://poetryprof.com/the-flower-fed-buffaloes/

The Owl and the Pussycat. Literary Devices. (accessed January 2021).
https://literarydevices.net/the-owl-and-the-pussy-cat/

Tearle, Oliver. A Short Analysis of Edward Lear's 'The Owl and the Pussycat'. Interesting Literature.   (accessed January 2021)
https://interestingliterature.com/2016/12/a-short-analysis-of-edward-lears-the-owl-and-the-pussycat/